James Hardison

# LET'S TOUCH
## HOW AND WHY TO DO IT

**A Touchstone Book**
Published by Simon & Schuster
New York   London   Toronto   Sydney   New Delhi

Touchstone
A Division of Simon & Schuster, Inc.
1230 Avenue of the Americas
New York, NY 10020

First Touchstone trade paperback edition July 2011

TOUCHSTONE and colophon are trademarks of Simon & Schuster, Inc.

For information about special discounts for bulk purchases,
please contact Simon & Schuster Special Sales at 1-866-506-1949
or business@simonandschuster.com.

The Simon & Schuster Speakers Bureau can bring authors to your live event.
For more information or to book an event contact the Simon & Schuster
Speakers Bureau at 1-866-248-3049 or visit our website at www.simonspeakers.com.

Designed by Frank Moorman

Manufactured in the United States of America

1   3   5   7   9   10   8   6   4   2

The Library of Congress has cataloged the Prentice-Hall edition as follows:
Hardison, James.
Let's touch.
(A Spectrum Book)
Bibliography : p. 215
Includes index.
1. Touch.  2. Interpersonal relations.  3. Emotions.  I. Title.
BF275.H29        152.1'82        80-18726

ISBN 978-0-1353-2812-5
ISBN 978-1-4516-6386-0 (pbk)

# Contents

Contents

Contents

To all who wish to enrich their lives through human touching for the purpose of improving learning and communication, and for giving and receiving recognition, consolation, understanding, appreciation, gratitude, empathy, friendship, profound love; and to all who have already enriched their own lives and the lives of those around them through touch.

# Preface

Touching is a natural form of human behavior. We all use it, consciously or otherwise, to create desired effects. It follows from this that we need to know what effects are desirable and how we create them through touching. Most research literature on touching is too technical to be interesting and understandable to anyone without a background in psychology or medicine. Touching research, however, does present many far-reaching implications of touch in our lives; the significance of touch is not limited to the sexual domain, as much popular literature would have us believe. This book describes the methods and principles of touching as identified in relevant research literature. It explains them accurately and understandably for use by members of the helping professions as well as the layman.

The book was written as a practical guide to understanding and improving touching for learning, relating, and attaining happiness. A greater emphasis is placed on how to do it with more meaning than on academic and theoretical issues. Thus, Part I, "The Touching Experience," covers the practical life experiences of touching, whereas Part II, "Touching Literature," synthesizes selected research and writing on human touching. Although the reader will inevitably find some chapters more provocative than others, I suggest they be read in sequence, for succeeding chapters are built upon earlier concepts.

# Acknowledgments

It is rewarding and simultaneously humbling to take an inventory of one's debts after writing such a book as this. I suddenly realize how many helpful friends and colleagues have made extensive contributions.

A reawakening to the value and importance of the sense of touch is owed to my granddaughter, Mandy Dutton, who at the age of two months was entrusted to me for two weeks of feeding, changing, bathing, and medicating.

Great encouragement, interest, and support were continually given me by colleagues too numerous to mention at San Diego Community College District and the California State Department of Education. Over the many months of preparing the first draft, Beverly Berwick of United States International University edited the writing and encouraged me to continue. For assistance in organizing and editing the first draft of the manuscript, I am grateful to Pat O'Dowd Jana, Janet Arundel, and Betty Eilerman.

The final draft would not have reached fruition without the reorganizing, editing, and guidance of Diane Marinelli, who demonstrated limitless patience, perseverance, tact, and refreshing insight. Typist Pat Bethel is to be commended for her cooperation and skill in preparing the final manuscript.

I must finally mention the enormous debt to all of my family, relatives, schoolmates, and friends; through the interchange of touch with them (most pleasant), I became aware of the importance of touching in my life. This, in a real sense, is as much their book as mine.

# PART ONE

# THE TOUCHING EXPERIENCE

# chapter one

# Touching:
# What's It All About?

Let's touch! We all do it, and we are doing it all the time. Yet few of us are conscious of how much touching we do. Stop and think about it. You are touching something at this moment. Notice your hands. What are they touching? Probably this book or some part of your own body. Part of you may be touching a chair. Your feet are touching the ground in some way. You are touching your clothes. To be in this world is to be constantly touching something.

What is touch, anyway? Did you ever stop to think about it? We use the terms *touch* and *touching* in a multitude of ways. Consider these expressions: "touchdown," "touching base," "a touch of madness," "a touching story," "I'm deeply touched." How many different connotations we give to *touch* in our everyday speech! But we still have not come up with a definition of the word.

Touch is one of the senses of the body. According to Gibson (1962), touching is an experience realized through the slightest indentation on the skin. This simple definition encompasses an extremely wide range of experiences, varying in intensity from the often unnoticed touch of a mosquito alighting on the arm in search of food to the severe blow received in a fistfight. How aware are you of the people and things that touch you? Have you thought about your own touching of people and things? Most of us haven't. We tend to take our touching for granted.

Touch is somewhat "the forgotten sense." We depend more on our eyes and ears, two "sets of receptors," for obtaining information about the world; and we rely on speech for sending out messages. But just think! Our whole bodies are capable of receiving messages through the "slightest indentation on the skin"! Such communication is in no way limited to the sexual realm. Why can't we more fully develop this potential?

We become aware of touching activities when the objects we touch give us a painful or pleasurable feeling. If we sit in one position or lean on one part of the body long enough to reduce the circulation, the affected part lets us know by aching or causing us pain. We then become acutely aware of the results of that touching activity and react by assuming a different position. We tend to react quickly to the accidental touching of extremely hot or cold objects. Thus, touching experiences, even in a negative way, play a significant role in our adaptability and learning. We adapt quickly and learn not to touch things that give our bodies a feeling of pain. Conversely, we seek out touching activities that give us pleasure.

We tend to repeat pleasurable touching experiences because they are so rewarding. We learn that touching our sore feet with warm water (not too hot) brings us a soothing, pleasurable feeling. We touch the cool (not too cold) wet sand with our feet on a warm sunny day, and we feel a delightful refreshment. By touching different parts of our bodies, we learn that there are some areas more sensitive and more pleasure giving than others. We progressively explore the body's reactions to the more pleasurable forms of touching and cultivate these over

**4**

the years. But why limit our conscious "touching life" to those moments when we are jolted into awareness by intense pleasure or pain?

As we grow from infancy to adulthood, we develop our own ideas about touching ourselves and others. For many of us, parental training taught that touching the self and others should be limited as much as possible. In our teenage years, permissible touching with parents included pats on the back and handshakes or hugs. Socially acceptable touching could include kissing on the cheek among girls and a goodnight kiss or two on a date. Among some generations, the only acceptable occasion for holding an opposite-sex partner was on the dance floor. Teenagers are not always convinced of the parental rules on touching and formulate rules of their own that would allow for self-exploration and discoveries of the opposite sex.

Unwritten rules of society have relegated touching activities primarily to sexual interaction or to aggression. These same rules have identified most touching, hugging, cuddling, or prolonged embracing behavior among adults exclusively as part of the sex act. Society's unwritten rules have announced "do not touch" and have left us with a fear of many meaningful types of touching. Thus, there is a taboo that prevents us from touching to improve communication. We are restrained from using touch to give and receive recognition, consolation, understanding, appreciation, gratitude, empathy, and friendship. There are even some limitations on the kinds of touch one can use to communicate profound love and caring to one's spouse. Unfortunately, we have placed an unchallenged set of limitations on our touching activities; these taboos, in many ways, have denied us our complete humanness.

This book investigates touching and its effects on our lives. It addresses the sociological, psychological, and physical needs for touching and how we might better use touching to gain and maintain more meaningful lives. Hopefully, our study will help us rid ourselves of the taboos associated with touching, so that

5

we can regain vital touching activities and use them to their fullest potential.

Thinking about touching requires a little imagination and a small amount of concentration. Mix the two together, and you become aware of what or whom you are touching and what or who is touching you. Try it right now. It's helpful to limit your incoming sight, so you may want to close your eyes for a minute. Now what are you touching? What are you feeling? What is touching you?

You might start with your face. Is there any breeze making "slight indentations on your skin"? Do you feel a fresh touch of air moving through your nasal passages, cooler going in and warmer coming out? Can you tell if the air touching the membranes in your nose feels dry or moist?

How about your clothes? Are there any elastic bands in your garments that press uncomfortably into your skin, cutting off the circulation? If you are wearing a belt, does it encircle your waistline loosely, or is it so tight that it sculpts a red ring around your middle? Are there any folds in your undergarments that, if left folded, may cause you some discomfort? Are your clothes comfortably hugging your body, or are they strangling you? Do they feel silky, soft, or rough?

How about your toes? Are they jammed together in fashionable shoes or enjoying freedom in more practical ones? Is the ground hard beneath your feet, or does a soft pillow gently support them?

We don't often focus on the touch sensations buzzing in our bodies—their messages are lost in the unconscious part of our minds. But with a little effort, we can become more aware of touches, respond to them more deliberately, and take control of our touching activity.

Touching is, however, both a physical and an emotional experience. We have a feeling reaction to the sensations we receive. We have this emotional response even in relation to things; for example, as we mentioned regarding clothes that fit snugly, we might experience this as a comfortable hugging or as strangulation.

There are two different types of touch: active and passive. In active touch, we initiate the experience. We actively touch persons or things in order to learn more about them or to communicate with them. Thus, we have the expression "to get in touch with" someone or something.

We explore objects by moving our hands over them. You might say we come to know objects more fully when we use the hands as sense organs. Active touching activates sense receptors in tendons and joints of the hand, bringing about a multitude of hand and finger positions. We gain greater definition and perception of visually perceived objects by running our fingers over them, back and forth. Our fingers are capable of tracing lines and shapes and other specific components of objects. Thus, active touch may be likened to visual scanning (Gibson 1962). It is used particularly well by the blind for gaining information about the world. If the blind can use active touch so well to learn about their immediate environment, then the sighted might imitate their approach to gain greater awareness of their world.

Active touch does not necessarily change our environment, but it can create a change in our perception of that environment. Consider any nearby object, like a pillow or another person's hands. By only looking at these objects, we have one perception of them. When we reach out and touch them, we don't change them, but we do change our perception of them: through touch we learn that the pillow is soft or hard, that the person's hands are smooth or rough, warm or cold.

Active touch, however, is not used solely for the purpose of expanding perception. We also use active touch for communicating. We can touch a person's arm to attract his or her attention. We can touch someone's hand in a light patting manner that conveys encouragement and support. There is also the possibility that we might send an active touching message to express encouragement and that the receiver may "read" the

7

message incorrectly as an amorous advance. This possible confusion of messages between sender and receiver brings us to a consideration of passive touch.

Passive touch is initiated by a source other than ourselves. Objects or persons coming into contact with our bodies initiate passive touch. Passive touch is part of the sensations realized through minor indentations and the slightest deformations of the skin when other objects or persons touch us. Whenever we place our hands under running water, slight indentations are made on the skin surfaces, and we receive the passive touch of the water running over our hands. A breeze blowing ever so lightly on the face alters the skin surface to advise of the passive touch from the breeze. When someone puts a hand on your shoulder, minor indentations are made, and you become involved in passively receiving the touch from the other person.

When we experience a touch passively that is, as a receiver—we attach some feeling reaction to it. We might experience the running water on our hands as pleasant and soothing, the breeze blowing on the face as refreshing, the touch to the shoulder as comforting and reassuring.

In the case of touching for communication, there is the possibility that the sender and receiver of the "touch message" may not both attach the same meaning to it. Rather than being comforting and reassuring, that touch to the shoulder could be interpreted as threatening or as suggestive of sexual attraction. Those "certain feelings" we associate with touching or being touched differ among individuals and frequently lead to misunderstandings. For effective communication, the intended message must be clarified by the sender.

There is a lot more to touching than indentations on the skin and active and passive roles. It is those "feelings," "meanings," and "interpretations" that make touching and being touched such individual experiences. No one else can know what a specific touch feels like to any one of us. Each of us has a unique history of touch experiences. There are, however, many things we can learn about touching. It is part of life—literally "from the womb to the tomb." In this book, we systematically look at the role of touch in different stages of human development—from conception through infancy, childhood, adolescence, adulthood, and the final stage of life. Touching has the potential to enrich our lives at each stage. So let's begin at the beginning.

Let's touch! Who does it naturally? Why, each and every one of us—as infants. We come into the world unable to see. Our speech is not developed. We can hear, but we cannot apply meaning to the sounds. What is our strongest sense?—the sense of touch. How do we survive? We learn survival skills by touching. What do we touch at this stage of life? We touch those persons and things that will satisfy our needs for food, for love. We touch those things that help us to learn about our environment and ourselves. At no other time is touching more crucial for physical and psychological development. And there is no time in our lives more filled with the delight found in touching and learning. We have no inhibitions about whom we touch or where we touch them. So when it comes to touching, each of us is a "natural-born" toucher. Chapter 2, "Young Touchings: Doing It Naturally," explores the natural touching activities of infant life. Early touching has beneficial effects upon later life. The consequences of touch deprivation have some serious implications for all of us. There is evidence that some infants have actually died from lack of touch. Hopefully, insights from this book will help prevent touch deprivations of this magnitude.

Around the fourth month of life, young muscles are ready to take us to new heights of exploration. We begin to move the body more deliberately. We are able to touch more of those things that have heretofore been out of reach. Before long, we become prolific touchers.

Why do we have to "touch everything" as we learn? How many of our mothers have posed this question in total exasperation? Why do we not heed the warning "Don't touch!"? We are

9

not yet able to incorporate abstract concepts into our sense of reality. In addition, since our speech is not fully developed during this period, we cannot express all our questions, and we lack clarity about the meaning of the words we hear. Yet we have a need to know things, and our surest way of knowing them is by touching them. As suggested on a popular children's television program, we need to "go ahead and touch, go ahead and feel; reach out and see if what you see is real." Chapter 3 explores touching from the perspective of childhood experiences—that touching makes things real. Such a perspective will enable us, in our dealings with children and with ourselves, to enhance and not thwart the desire to learn by touching.

Who can touch whom? When? Where? How? For how long? Taboos are those "little rules," mostly unwritten, that society has drawn up to regulate touching activities. Taboos tell us not to touch our bodies or the bodies of our loved ones. They also set limits on how long we can hold on to a handshake, a kiss, or a hug. There are, or at least there once were, reasons for all the taboos. But do they continue to serve our needs as individuals and as a society? Or do they prevent us from using touching in many meaningful ways? How can we get loose from such constraints? The first step is to identify these societal "rules" that we take for granted and examine them "in the light of day." Chapter 4, "Taboos About Touching: Tracking Them Down," will assist you in taking this step and gaining a new perspective on your potential for using touch in a wholesome, human way.

How aware are you of yourself? How can you get to know more about yourself, so you can understand yourself better and possibly even like yourself more? We learn about our bodies and ourselves through self-touching. We also get to know ourselves by touching others and seeing the way they react to our touch. Moreover, we can learn about ourselves by the way others touch us and the reactions we have to their touches. Research suggests that those of us who are "touchers" and allow ourselves to be touched by others become more aware of ourselves and the world around us. Why do "touchers" have a better chance for self-awareness? They tend to gain more confidence and trust in their relationships with others and thus open up to more trusting communication with them. Chapter 5, "Touching for Self-Awareness," describes some perhaps surprising ways that "touchers" have an edge on the rest of us.

The tactual experience, serving to locate a person in time and space, can help us to establish a foundation for higher-order operations. It is our constant contact with the earth that gives us a reassuring sense of support; the earth is our stable referent. We explore in this book how touching and being touched identify us in time and space and allow us to establish a firm and secure foundation from which to manage our lives.

What does touching have to do with communication?—a great deal! It is the means of communication we use very effectively when some circumstance limits our use of words. During the first two years of life, we depend primarily on touching as our means of communication. In later life, we seem to revert back to touching for communication as our hearing and speech deteriorate. The human skin, a fascinating receptor of communications, is in the limelight as a primary and terminal sense organ. Chapter 6, "Touching for Communication," describes how we can learn to use touching to enhance our communication throughout life. We can use it to express concern, recognition, understanding, affection, love, and many more of the subtle and profound messages we wish to convey.

Research has indicated that touching is crucial to interpersonal relationships, perhaps even more significant than verbal communication. What does a touch communicate to the various individuals we encounter in our lives? How can we make sure that our friendly touches are interpreted correctly by the receiver? The act of touching and being touched transcends the separateness of existence. We can be freed from the taboos against touching and can use it to bring about a feeling of

**11**

oneness with others. Chapter 7, "Touching for Improving Interpersonal Relationships," explores the delicate questions of when, where, and how to use touch effectively with a relative, friend, or associate of either sex.

How do we best demonstrate our affection with infants and children?—by touching! We use touching for loving both the little people and the big people. Touch is loving, and love is touching for persons of any age. Yet so many of us abuse and misuse touch for other goals and purposes. Why do we use touch in demeaning and controlling ways? Each of us applies touching in loving interactions for different reasons. Some of us touch our partners to express endearment. Others touch their mates exclusively to arouse them. Can you enjoy your loved one by touching just for the joy of touching? Or do you touch only to say that you want to have sex? Chapter 8, "Touching for Loving and Making Love," delves into the vast research of the past three decades that addresses the issues of how and when to use touch to enhance your love life *and* your sex life. Why not take up the challenge of becoming a better toucher in all the loving encounters in your life?

Most of us know, at least subconsciously, that touching can bring happiness. Can you think of any occasion when you felt an inner need or sense of incompleteness and attempted to assuage it by reaching out to touch someone or something? It may have been your spouse, or your child, or a favorite object, or a pet. Probably you did not do it consciously. Such an experience is very natural. Somehow, just being in physical contact with people or even things we are fond of is rewarding. It can even be a healing experience.

Currently, there is a revival of interest in touching for healing, or "touch therapy." Can touch actually be used to restore health to a person? Chapter 9 addresses both the common experience of touching for being happy and the deliberate therapeutic use of touch for healing.

How do you start your own touching program? Can you

change your present touching patterns? How difficult is it to touch with meaning? A small word of caution is in order. If you are interested in going all out for a touching program that can change your life, don't jump into it blindfolded. Let people know what you are doing before you come across as "handling" them. That can kill your enthusiasm as well as theirs. People generally expect us to behave the way we usually do. When we come across with something different, particularly if it means putting our "paws" on them when we have never done it before, they need some preparation beforehand. Tell them what the touch means to you before you apply it. Otherwise, they may get some "funny" idea about you and what you are up to. The final chapter in Part I, "Let's Start Touching: Here's How to Do It," offers some basic suggestions on how to start, when to start, and whom to start with. Each of us approaches a new behavior pattern in a different way. Hopefully, the chapter will help you find your own unique way to a rewarding and meaningful use of touching in your life.

What do psychologists really know about human touching? Research on this topic is relatively new. Over the past ten years, however, researchers have taken great strides in exploring the significance of human touch. Part II of *Let's Touch*, "Touching Literature," briefly summarizes many of the theories and studies that currently make up the literature on this subject.

# chapter two

# Young Touchings: Doing It Naturally

An infants, we depend on touch for our physical and psychological development. We are uninhibited in our touching behavior, since it is primarily instinctual at this stage in our lives. But before exploring our infant touchings, we take a look at the essential role of touch in our development prior to birth.

## Conception

Human life begins as a result of touching. Man sexually touches woman; their genitals are involved in profound touching activities; the penis touches the inside linings and folds of the female reproductive canal. The sperm spring forth, touching the lower walls of the vagina and the cervix. Destiny directs one sperm out of millions to the ovum; when the two touch, they become one. This contact begins a new life. Survival of the new life in embryo form depends upon its ability to locate and attach itself to the lining of the womb. Clearly, the value of touch and touching are most significant to the beginning of our very existence.

## In the Womb

Secured to the lining of the womb and nurtured by this contact, the human embryo develops the first of its senses, the sense of touch (McCorkle, 1974). The amniotic fluids and the extended walls of the womb make up the tactual environment for the new life. The embryo feels the maternal hearbeat as the vibrations pass through the fluids and gently stimulate the newly forming skin surfaces (McCorkle 1974). The tactual sensations of the unborn child become his or her first orientation to the mother and to life. This contact, this feeling of oneness with the mother, is the foundation of the human need for touching throughout life. In the womb we experience a nine-month period of cuddling and a closeness of unequaled security. Impressions of this lengthy tactual experience are undoubtedly recorded in our brains. If we could trace these faint early impressions that told us to some degree what living was going to be like, they would surely recall a happy tranquility. We all have a subsequent desire to reconstruct a similar environment outside the womb. After having experienced a natural closeness inside the womb, we continue to seek this closeness, this cuddling touch, throughout life.

## Birth

In the birth process, massive contractions of the uterus upon our newly formed bodies activate our vital life systems. Uterine contractions are the primal touching activity that prepares the body to begin an independent life outside the womb. The tight, bandlike pulsations of the uterus move across the head and abdomen in sustained and released touches as we begin our movement out of the birth canal. Ashley Montagu (1971) refers to the uterine contractions of labor as the "beginning caressing of the baby in the right way—a caressing which should be continued in very special ways in the period immediately following birth and for a considerable time thereafter." This touching action stimulates the body and, in doing so, enables it to function independently in the outside world. The birth canal is about four inches in length. Sometimes it takes us six or eight hours or more to travel through the canal. As we make our way, ever so slowly, the skin and body receive the hugging touches of the womb. Uterine hugs stimulate the nerves in our skin. A chain reaction occurs as the nerve endings in the skin pass the stimulation to the central nervous system, which, in turn, passes stimulations to the vital systems that control our breathing, blood circulation, digestion, excretion, and brain function.

If for some reason we do not experience the hugging sensations of passing through the birth canal, we may experience some developmental disadvantages. Those of us who are taken from the mother's body by caesarean section (c-section) fall into this category. Also, those of us who are born prematurely are less likely to receive as much tactual stimulation in passing through the birth canal as a full-term baby. Due to the lack of touching sensations in birth, such children may experience difficulty in breathing, greater lethargy, and less responsiveness to stimulation, not only just after birth but throughout life. Premature and caesarean-born children may also have a higher incidence of nose and throat infections. They tend to experience delayed development of bladder and bowel control as well as of language and manual skills and are generally less adaptive and more easily upset than full-term infants delivered through the birth canal. As a result, premature and caesarean-born children are more likely to experience temper tantrums, restlessness, personality difficulties, and fear of school (Montagu 1971).

This sounds like bad news if we are premature or caesarean-born! But there are other factors that can work to offset this early lack of touching. Massaging the infant directly after premature or c-section delivery offers great promise as a substitute for the massage effect produced by the contractions of the uterus. No scientific evidence is yet available as to the long-term effect of postnatal massage, but many physicians are recommending extensive body massage for both c-section and natural-born infants. Dr. Paul Brenner, a San Diego physician is taking greater interest in massage than most members of the profession. He is reported to have established a routine of postnatal infant massage. Mothers are trained to feel and massage their infants several times during the day. First unofficial reports of the effects are positive. Infants receiving these massages are apparently, whether delivered by c-section or natural birth, more responsive to stimuli, less restless, and less apt to demonstrate ill temper.

## Bonding

Bonding—what is it? It is the unique link of a mutually satisfying relationship between a mother and her newborn baby. Immediate bonding of the mother with her newborn infant offers important psychological and physical benefits to each.

The mother needs the infant as much as the infant needs the mother. If the contact with her child is not continued, the mother will feel a void, a sense of emptiness, an emotional experience of not being fulfilled. If the newborn child is placed on the mother's body after delivery, the child can hear the mother's heartbeat, a source of comfort and security because it is a familiar sound, heard while in the womb. The continuation of close physical contact between them is significant in many ways. The mother and the child have been in constant contact with each other during pregnancy. They have felt the awareness of each other; their continual body contact has been a source of comfort to each. They have experienced the immediate presence and assurance gained from being in contact with another human being. The child in the womb is in a state of comfort from the maternal warmth. A disruption of the continuum of contact between the two at birth is a disruption of intimacy, a startling shock to their sense of security. The upset of this separation can be eased by close body contact after delivery.

The mother and her newborn child truly need each other for continued physical development as well as for emotional stability. The body of the mother has been nine months in preparation to fill her role in delivering and feeding the child. The child's growth over the same period results in a state of absolute dependency upon the mother outside the womb for feeding and care. After delivery, the infant is in immediate need of the early maternal milk, colostrum, in the mother's breast. This form of breast milk lasts for only two or three days. Immediately sucking colostrum will prevent the newborn from having diarrhea. Immediate nursing also benefits the mother: it causes the uterus to return more quickly and naturally to its normal state.

The physical and mental development of the newborn baby requires frequent and close contact with the mother. This contact elicits from the baby the sensitivity and awareness needed to foster learning and physical growth. Bonding resulting from early close contact appears to influence the baby's weight gain positively and to result in few infections up through the first year of life. In addition to these physical benefits, bonding results in an intuitive understanding between mother and child whereby the mother instinctively knows what the child wants and reacts accordingly. This psychological bond reduces the number of words spoken by the mother to the growing child; it requires the bonding mother to give fewer commands than nonbonding mothers give to their toddlers. This mother–child understanding reduces the tension of the "terrible twos and threes." The bonding mother can be less forbidding and restricting with her child and more supportive of learning experiences. The result for the child is greater psychological development, higher IQ, and significantly greater langauge test scores in later years (Galton 1978).

In a psychological sense, there is also a bonding that occurs between a newborn baby and his or her father. The father, after waiting nine months to see and touch the "new creation," is in need of contact with the infant. Seeing and, particularly, holding the infant that is a part of his creation evoke the pride and joy of being a father. As the months of pregnancy have rolled by, the father has witnessed the growth of the mother's abdomen. This, in part, is a confirmation of his role as a parent. Feeling the fetus is another confirmation that he has been a participant in the starting of a new life. The father is anxious to see and feel the reality of that new life. Thus, when the infant first arrives, preferably during delivery and immediately following, the father's presence allows him to share in the arrival of what he has helped to create. It allows the father to confirm fully his paternal role from the very beginning. Touching and holding the newborn infant bring the earlier expectations to reality and answer the questions, "Will it be a boy or girl?" and "Will it be healthy and delivered safely?" When the father observes or assists in the delivery, these questions can be best answered firsthand by his own observation and participation. For those fathers who are the first human beings to pick up their infants and cuddle them, the joy of touching the new life becomes a peak experience that carries with it emotional ties drawing out the paternal sense of protection and caring.

Siblings can also develop a bonding with newborn infants through touch. Such sibling bonding is helpful because it brings out feelings that limit jealousy and facilitate communication from the start (Galton 1978).

The tactual bonds we establish with our mothers and fathers have long-term beneficial consequences. Bonding experiences during the first few months of life play an important role in the formation of the personality. Our earliest touch experiences set up a pattern for later expectation. We begin to develop an attitude toward ourselves from these experiences, and we tend to hold as valid our first attitude about them. If we enjoy our touches, we tend to like ourselves. Our attitude toward our parents will be one of either warmth or hostility, based primarily on our touch experience with them. If we form an early hostile attitude toward a parent, we may be carrying that hostile feeling around with us, even though on a subconscious level, for an entire lifetime. If we first view our parents' touches as "controlling" instead of as offering an opportunity for independence, we may become "bonded" to the parents as being "controlling", and later in life the bond is difficult to break.

The implications of these early bonding experiences are particularly significant during the teenage years. Our attitude toward ourselves and our relationship with our parents go through considerable growing pains in adolescence. If these attitudes are healthy ones to start with, we will have a good foundation for optimal growth. In addition, touching contact with the mother, particularly within the first few hours, has a great influence on our ability to participate in loving sexual relationships in later life.

Fortunately, it appears that early contacts and touching activities with newborn infants are increasing. Hospital staff and physicians have begun to take steps to see that there are greater opportunities for mothers and fathers to be in closer contact with their newborn infants. In some places, hospitals are providing birthing rooms, where both parents spend the first hours with their new baby in a homelike setting instead of the usual segregation of recovery room and nursery. In such places, provision is being made for the father to assist in the delivery, cut the umbilical cord, and bathe his newborn child. Although long-term studies of the effects of such a birth experience are not yet available, current reports of the apparent effects on both parents and offspring are very positive (Galton 1978).

## Feeding

Our touching behavior as infants appears to be automatic and instinctual, and it serves our most basic needs: the need for nourishment, for physical stimulation, and for the warmth and security of being loved. Let us now take a look at feeding as it relates to these needs.

As infants, we have a built-in ability to search for food; this behavior is referred to as *rooting*. This type of touching behavior is characteristic of the infant stage in that it is so instinctual. Principally, we use the lips and mouth to root as a means of locating a food source. Our highly sensitive lips serve as tactual scanners. They move across the breast until we find the source of food. Our lips explore, moving up and down, in and out, until our tongue feels the satisfying, warm maternal milk. The flow of milk into the mouth brings our rooting behavior to a stop, and we direct our full attention and energy to nursing. Initially a highly mechanical, sometimes almost frantic, machinelike approach to scanning the mother's chest, breast, and nipple, rooting behavior gradually takes on a smoother, more rational manner, including an even scanning and locating of the nurturing nipple. The sucking activity becomes calm and more purposeful, as if we now know that this oral contact will bring the food we seek.

An infant's lips have a built-in need for tactual stimulation. When the infant sucks upon the mother's breast, this need is met, and the need anxiety is reduced or progressively satisfied. This need for oral stimulation is related to the need for food but extends beyond it; therefore, it is natural for infants to enjoy sucking activity for its own sake. The lips and tongue are among those parts of the body with an extremely high concentration of sense receptors (the tongue, in fact, has the highest concentration). Oral touching experiences in infancy bring us the sophistication of muscle control and sensitivity we need for later speech development and for using the lips in lovemaking as adults.

21

Breast-feeding, as a function of bonding, brings the mother and child into an emotional and social interaction. The child is given the opportunity to experience body contact with the mother, a contact that gives security while it provides tactual stimulation and relief of hunger. In a very real sense, we need the cuddling and loving touches we receive during feeding as much as the physical nourishment. Breast-feeding also helps to socialize us. It helps us to learn to interact with another person during feeding. The implications are long lasting. If the bonding through breast-feeding is rewarding for infant and mother, we will associate pleasurable social relations with eating periods and seek them out in later life.

The experience of breast-feeding an infant is significant for the mother herself. It is a giving of herself in an affectionate way both physically and emotionally. The mother fulfills the biological purpose of her breasts; she provides the milk to the sucking infant. The flow of milk to her infant releases the pressures of the ducts containing the life-supporting milk. The infant's gentle sucking is a recognition and confirmation of her maternal role. No other experience confirms motherhood with such poignant pleasure. The touch of the infant's lips and mouth is an assurance to the mother that she is necessary in nurturing her infant and is linked to the continuity of humanity. Breast-feeding is also a social experience between the mother and the child, a time for interacting. It enables the mother to recognize any change in the physical condition or mood of her infant. Through this close contact, the mother can feel a rise in her infant's temperature. The infant also communicates to the mother a state of anxiety or contentment by the "mood" of the sucking. An anxiously hungry infant will suck impatiently and attempt to take on more milk over a shorter period of time than the calm infant who sucks gently over longer periods of time. In all, the infant's sucking touches to the nipple and breast bring the mother a warm pleasure and direct communication with her child that she receives in no other way.

Ordinarily, bottle-feeding is less conducive to bonding than breast-feeding. The reason for this is that in many cases, the bottle-fed infant, receives less cuddling and body contact than the breast-fed infant. A mother can give her infant a bottle without having to hold the baby during the entire feeding. The infant can feed himself or herself from a propped-up bottle; in such a case, the child interacts with another person only at the beginning and end of the feeding period and for burping. For mothers who choose to bottle-feed their children, it is preferable that the child always be held and fondled during feeding as a means of communicating the feelings of affection and security that are so conducive to healthy physical and psychological development.

## Love and Security Needs

When we are newborns, hands are touching us to feed, bathe, rock, and comfort us. Touching and being touched are the key to our earliest communication. We depend upon this nonverbal means of communiction until we develop verbal capabilities. Our mothers pick us up and cuddle us when we become upset. They talk to us in reassuring words we do not yet understand. Their touches and cuddling tell us in a nonverbal way that we are secure and have no need to be upset. The warmth and tenderness of the mother's body communicates to us, as did her womb, that we are in a safe place.

During this stage of life, we begin to develop expectations that are internalized according to the rate and frequency with which our needs are met. If our cries are met promptly and we are usually patted, burped, changed, or fed without excessive delay, we learn to expect that attention and relate it to the degree of caring others have for us. On the other hand, if we receive no response or substantially delayed responses to our whimpers and cries of discomfort, we begin to build up the feeling that we are little valued, little loved. For this reason, it cannot be overemphasized that the time of infancy is crucial in formulating expectancies of loving and being loved. The body is highly receptive because it is at this point that we are our most open, responsive, and vulnerable selves. Without reservation, we are ready to learn to love. Especially if we are cuddlers, we respond positively to holding, stroking, fondling, and hugging by clinging, snuggling, making contented sounds, or just peacefully falling asleep. As we grow, we become more responsive to the attention we receive, and with increasing deliberateness, we snuggle up to the body that is holding us. We love attention and respond to playful stimulation by involuntarily swatting our playmate in the face or on the arm, or by kicking him or her in the stomach—whatever our spontaneous reaction causes us to do. Such loving exchanges as these are essential for our emotional and social development.

## Cuddlers and Noncuddlers

Were you a cuddler or a noncuddler as an infant? So many of us assume that all babies are cuddlers. One would think that after nine months of being securely cuddled in the womb, we would all seek our favorite cuddling position in a mother's arms. Not so, say the researchers (Schaffer and Emerson 1964). Not all infants are cuddlers. Some infants resist cuddling interaction with their mothers under most conditions and circumstances. The noncuddler pattern may continue through their eighteenth month without modification, even at times of fear, pain, or illness. It is highly possible that the noncuddler infant found the womb too confining for some yet-to-be-discovered reasons and, as a result, developed a resistance to the cuddling posture. One study reported a contrast between cuddlers and noncuddlers: cuddler infants sought a caressing touch as a diversion during times of stress, whereas noncuddler infants accepted a bottle or biscuit as a means of distraction (Schaffer and Emerson 1964).

Noncuddling in itself is not bad; it is a problem, though, in those cases where the mother is incapable of using alternate ways of relating to the infant. Noncuddlers do not avoid contact altogether. On the contrary, they accept being tickled or having the face stroked (without being picked up) as much as the cuddlers. They also actively accept being swung, romped with, or bounced—almost any method of contact that does not include restraint (Schaffer and Emerson 1964). Actually, it is not the touching that noncuddlers wish to avoid but any holding activity that restricts their movements while being cuddled. Infants who demonstrate a strong resistance to cuddling often mislead their parents into thinking they do not want or need to be touched. Many parents consequently hold back on touching their infants and tend to deprive them unnecessarily of this vital stimulation and communication of love.

Specifically, noncuddlers resist intimate touching; yet they seek out limited forms of contact, like those exhibited in rocking and rough play, for consolation. Parents of noncuddlers should recognize that from the age of six months on, noncuddlers exhibit a greater dislike for being changed, wrapped, or dressed than do cuddlers.

Cuddlers and noncuddlers do eventually become discriminating in their need for tactile attention. At approximately nine months of age, cuddlers begin to demonstrate a need for contact and proximity with specific persons. Noncuddlers are slower to develop this trait. When noncuddlers first establish a tie to specific persons, the bond tends to be weak. By the time cuddlers and noncuddlers reach the eighteenth month, differences in their touching behavior patterns diminish.

## Touch Deprivation

Infants can easily be deprived of fundamental forms of touching when they are matched with nontouching mothers. Fortunately, touch deprivation from the mother is frequently replaced by comforting contact with other family members. Frequently, older brothers and sisters provide significant loving touches. Siblings or other parent substitutes who provide the needed touching when the mother fails to do so are very important for the physical and psychological development of infants who would otherwise be stunted.

What are the effects of touch deprivation? In minor cases, touch deprivation consists of a significant lack of the physical and psychological advantages that are promoted by wholesome tactual stimulation. In the most severe cases, as a study of institutionalized infants showed, touch deprivation can result in death. The infants who had very limited contact with human stimulation developed a condition referred to as *marasmus*. As part of this condition, the youngsters would not respond to feeding, and they exhibited listlessness and general disease. They had a yellowish-gray pallor, lack of eye fluids, faint heartbeat, and shallow breathing. Beyond a certain point, some of these infants would not respond to any kind of touching and ultimately died (Montagu 1971).

## Lifelong Consequences

Unquestionably, the benefits of early touching experiences are realized throughout life. Touching fosters our growth as infants and children: those of us who receive the most physical contact from parents, siblings, or parent substitutes walk and talk earlier than others. The loving touches we receive as infants have an effect on our feelings and behavior. The stimulation of early touching experiences is an essential physiological basis for intellectual development. If our touching experiences during the first months of life are happy ones, we are likely to develop a strong sense of security, self-awareness, self-acceptance, and self-worth; we will also have the feeling of being recognized and loved and the ability to love others. These inner qualities will benefit us throughout life. Our verbal communication in later life and our ability to relate socially tend to reflect our early touching relationships. Satisfying touching experiences during infancy, especially with the mother, lay the foundation for rewarding sexual relationships in adulthood, because it is in our intimate touching interactions as infants that we learn to be comfortable in physically relating to another human being.

# chapter three

# Young Touchings: Learning through Exploration

Are we by nature explorers? What is the relationship between touching, exploring, and learning? Are there specific faculties we must have in order to become the energetic, tactual explorers we seem to become? What motivates us to reach and grab, to crawl and climb, and eventually to walk? What role does touching play in each of these activities? At what time in our young lives are we able to start an active tactual exploration of the self and the environment?

## Instinctual Responses to Touch

As newborn infants, we are highly responsive to touches in an instinctual way. When touched on the cheeks or lips, we instinctively open the mouth and move it toward the source of the touch. Upon being touched directly above the lips, we respond by opening the mouth and moving the head from side to side. It seems as if we have a "built-in search mode" triggered by touch for locating the nipple and placing it in the mouth. These responses are basic reflexes. Specific touches bring specific responses. Our reflex responses to touch are a part of our original makeup: we don't have to learn how to respond—we do it naturally. The conditions for these reflex responses are contingent upon good health and normal physiological development. Natural reflexes are the foundation for building learned behavior.

Just as reflex responses to touches near the mouth enable us to find our source of nourishment, other instinctual responses during infancy result in our ability to reach, grab, crawl, and walk. When our bent arms are pulled straight down and then released, we immediately return them to their angled position. This reflex response is fundamental to our ability to reach out and bring objects closer to the body; it enables us to learn by examining things at close range. Another basic reflex response is that of grasping. When triggered by a touch to the palm of the hand, this reflex causes us to close the fingers and thumb around the object and hold it tightly. Through the arm reflex and the hand-grasping reflex, we are intrinsically prepared for reaching out and learning about our world.

Just as our ability to reach out and grab is built upon instinctual response patterns, so our ability to crawl and walk is rooted in an innate reflex. As infants, our legs rest naturally in a bent position. When someone straightens out the legs and then suddenly releases them, we respond by bringing them back to their original bent position. This basic reflex is crucial in learning to extend the legs and flex them back to effect a crawling or walking mode.

Parents can confirm our potential for future learning by simply testing these reflexes, even during the first weeks of life.

## Readiness for Learning

Each stage of muscular and tactual development brings with it a corresponding optimal learning stage. Thus we have optimal periods for learning various physical maneuvers, such as grasping objects, crawling, and so on. We can still learn behaviors once the optimal period has passed, but it may not be as easy for us to do so. Development of muscles and nerves occurs at a rapid pace in the first six months of life. During this time, we experience what is probably our most crucial learning period. It is very important that our parents provide the appropriate stimulation and opportunities for learning during this phase.

During infancy, our eyesight gradually improves so that we can focus more effectively on things around us. Improving vision spurs our learning because it brings attractive objects to our attention. Bright colors and novel objects fascinate us and motivate us to reach out to touch and grab. As human beings, we all have a need for novelty. Even in the first six months of life, we demonstrate this need. In fact, the experience of novelty at this time is a vital necessity if we are to get off to a healthy start in neurological development. Our nerves and brain cells need lots of stimulation, both visual and tactual.

## Ability to Reach Out and Touch

Usually during the fourth month of life, we undergo a dramatic change: we begin to shift from predominantly instinctual responses to touch to initiating active physical interchanges. Up to this time, our source of gratification has been sucking—principally centered on the mother, the nipple, and the thumb. At this point, we begin to seek gratification from touching and learning; we enter the manual phase of exploration (White 1975). Any object within an arm's length, including the mother's face, is subjected to our first investigative swats. Our hands, heretofore held in a drawn-up, fisted position, become more noticeably unflexed. Although we reach out for objects in our range of vision, we are not yet quite able to grab hold of them. By the fifth month, however, we can reach out and grasp objects within easy reach. More specifically, we begin to demonstrate our first form of intelligent behavior that requires the use of combined muscular systems. We learn to execute a sequence of coordinated actions: (1) we move our arms and hands to the specific location of a target object; (2) we spread our hands to a width sufficient for grasping the object; and (3) we bring the object closer to the body for more effective tactual and visual examination. We are not yet able to hold objects between the thumb and fingers.

The manual phase of exploration is coupled with oral exploration; the objects that attract our manual examination will also be given the oral exploration test of sucking, gumming, chewing, and a wide variety of lip action (White 1975). Any object in the mouth, even a thumb or part of our fist, brings a sense of pleasure that is sometimes accompanied by a feeling of security. The high concentration of sense receptors on the lips and tongue, plus the sore gum tissue covering emerging baby teeth, helps explain why babies tend to put so many objects in their mouths (Burton and Heller 1964).

Another significant development during the fourth month of life is oral-tactual discrimination. We begin to distinguish between those objects that will bring us food and those that will not. If, in the course of oral explorations, we are gumming a rattle and our mother presents the breast or bottle, we quickly redirect our attention and are attracted to the source of nourishment. By this time, we have learned that the breast or bottle will give us more pleasure and satisfaction, particularly hunger reduction, than other attractive objects. These preferential selections are indicators of our earliest learning achievements and reflect a great change from the instinctive behavior of the first few weeks. We show that we can differentiate oral contact as a means of exploration and pleasure seeking from oral contact as a means of obtaining food.

Prior to the age of six months, we become hand-patters. We pat our hands together; we pat the table, the chair, we may even pat our parents on the head, face, or any part of the body within reach. This is followed by an interest in banging objects like spoons or cups against the table or tray of our high chair.

At six months, our eye-hand coordination has developed sufficiently for us to be able to reach for an object without looking directly at it. At an earlier age, we raked our hand along a surface to locate and pick up an object. At this point, we are able to go directly to an object, grasp it, and bring it toward us. We can hold objects more firmly than ever before, and we experience no difficulty in holding toys, turning them around, and passing them from one hand to the other.

By our sixth month we are able to demonstrate some understanding of permanence. We search for hidden objects. If someone shows us a toy and then hides it, we will lift up coverings or other things that obstruct our view and reach for it with confidence.

The fifth and sixth months are high growth months; this is a time, perhaps more than any other, when we should have many opportunities to touch and feel things. If we are physically ready to reach out and grab dangling toys and other objects and none are available to practice reaching for, then we may experience a lack of development at an optimal time and have greater difficulty later in learning this tactual exploration technique. We may have to make additional attempts to reach out and grab before we are successful.

Assuming that we have fully developed our tactile skills of grabbing and holding objects by the seventh month, we are ready to apply the skill to the practical application of feeding ourselves. We take to fingering foods. We have grabbed, held, and placed many objects in the mouth up to this point, not caring—as our mothers will attest—whether they were food or not. In our seventh month, we have the capability of fingering crackers, toast, and other edibles, touching them to the mouth and savoring them. During this same period we experience many trials and errors in learning, as we may not get all the cracker in the mouth, or we may find that it fits into the mouth with greater ease if entry is made with the cracker on a horizontal plane. It is during this period that we, having learned to hold an object in each hand simultaneously, take on the challenge of holding a cup or glass with both hands and attempting to guide it to our lips. This is one of the most complex operations we have attempted up to this point. The first attempts may not be completely successful.

At the age of eight months, we begin to indicate a preference for using one hand more than another. Some of use use both hands equally for another two or three months, but normally we have selected a preferred hand for tactile interaction by the twelfth month. A refinement also occurs in our selection of objects. Through the trial-and-error method, we are now relatively proficient in distinguishing which objects are the right size to hold in our hands. As we move through the eighth to twelfth months, our little fingers are more inquisitive than ever before. We use them to explore and help us learn about everything in sight.

Playing with clothespins is a good exercise for developing the use of the fingers, particularly the thumb in opposition to the fingers. With each pinch, we improve the strength and coordination of our thumb and finger muscles. Another good exercise, which strengthens our arm muscles, is throwing a ball.

## Mobility

Being able to move about independently is essential to our ability to learn through exploration. Prior to the fourth month of life, we have very little control over our posture and position in space. The head, if touching the bed in a resting position, controls the curvature of the rest of the body; our arms and legs follow suit. If we are resting with our right cheek touching the bed, we flex the left arm and extend the right arm. This stance leaves the body in an asymmetrical position, usually with our legs in a sprinter's stance. Interestingly enough, some time after the fourth month, we tend to prefer symmetrical body positions, leaving the head centered in relationship to the body, with our limbs slightly flexed. It is from this symmetrical position that we gain better balance with greater hand and body control; we then develop the strength in our arms and legs that will later give us the confidence and support needed to sit and stand.

Our self-initiated mobility begins during our third month. At this stage, from a position of lying on our stomach, we can use the hands and arms to raise our chest up from the bed. Soon after this, we learn to roll from stomach to side and then all the way over to our back. Between the sixth and ninth months, we learn to roll from the back to the stomach. Being new at learning to change, we occasionally overshoot the mark, and our sheer force and weight bring us to an unexpected position. Yet the experience expands our sense of tactual exploration, since it brings us closer to the tantalizing objects that have previously been out of touching range.

By the sixth month, we can assume a standing position, but our leg and arm muscles do not yet permit us to stand independently even when we are holding onto a supporting object. We sometimes experience frustration because we are unable to reach an object that is visually attractive. When we are held up with our feet just above the ground, we instinctively stretch our toes to the ground. This is not suggestive that we are ready to walk. We are just flexing the muscles that we will use later.

As many of our parents or caretakers will confirm, eight to twelve months is the beginning of a period of high mobility. We are able to pull ourselves over the floor in any of a number of ways. Some of us are on all fours; others scoot along, sitting in an upright position. This new mobility allows us to come within touching distance of those attractive and interesting-looking things that were formerly out of touching range. The muscles we developed in the playpen are ready for wider-range exploration. Greater opportunity for touching objects through creeping and crawling, even though it brings an increase in the admonition "Don't touch," stimulates our mental development. Once we start pulling ourselves to our feet and holding onto furniture or playpen to maintain the stance, everything in sight and reasonable reach becomes fair game for grasping, grabbing, turning around, over, and upside down. This list is almost unending. We tug at curtains, dresses, slacks, tablecloths, and drawers. How well we pursue the tactile search at this age is an indicator of our curiosity and alertness.

Some time between our twelfth and eighteenth months, we learn to walk alone. Look out world: here we come!

## Our Need to Touch

Our increasing ability to get around alone and our desire to touch the things that strike our interest create quite a challenge for our parents. But the new touching opportunities produce sheer delight in us, the tiny explorers. We explore objects—stroking, poking, squeezing, slapping, enfolding with mouth and hands—seemingly driven by an uncontrollable instinct to learn by touching. Among the two most sensitive areas of the body are the pads of the fingers and the tip of the tongue. Little wonder that we use our fingers and mouths to do a large amount of testing, trying out, feeling, and general sensing of the environment. The sensation of touching is stimulating and exciting; it makes us want to touch even more. Not only is it natural for us to do so, but it is most crucial for our development. Our inner drive to touch is so strong that we frequently ignore the "Don't touch!" Wise parents will create an environment where we have a certain amount of space in which to roam and where we can touch a variety of objects without getting hurt. Parents who do not make such a provision frustrate us and themselves when they repeat the admonition that we do not, indeed cannot, heed.

## Touch Facilitates Language Development

During the first two years of life and for some time afterward, our speech faculty is developing. We first learn the meaning of words spoken to us; the words we hear gradually come to symbolize the concepts and messages they are meant to communicate. Initially, these meanings are quite vague, but with time and experience, we come to understand more and more precisely what the words we hear really mean. Because our abstract concepts are not yet fully developed, words are not the most effective means of learning during the first years of life. Touching, feeling, concretely testing things out for ourselves—these are much more viable learning modes. We are truly eager to "know" about the things around us, and so we reach out to touch them. Touching makes things real.

As adults, we take abstract concepts for granted. We learn the meaning of these concepts in a very natural and unconscious way during early childhood, particularly through touching. During infancy we learn the difference between what is food and what is not food through repeated experiences with eating and feeling the hunger pains disappear, in contrast to sucking or chewing on something that is not food and feeling the hunger persist.

It is through touching that we learn what is and what is not part of the body. Even at the age of three or four months, we discover our hands and feet. At six or seven months, we are likely to discover the genital area and explore it with interest. The sensations we experience in touching our own bodies in contrast to those of touching other things, gradually teach us the limits of the body, and we begin to identify who we are.

One of the most fascinating concepts we learn is that of

36

water. Opportunities for being in contact with water are almost limitless. Significant contact with water began before we were born; we were partially suspended in the warm sea of fluids in the uterus. Seeking to renew this experience, we are attracted to warm baths, puddles, and swimming pools. In our first weeks of life, we learn about dampness through the discomfort of a wet diaper. In splashing bath water, we realize that the touch of our hands can influence the environment. Splashing is also one of our first activities on initiating play. Water is a lot of fun: we slap, swirl it, toss it up, let it drip, pour it out, squirt it, and float our toys in it. When we place it in jars, bottles, and pans of all sizes and shapes, we learn that unlike most other objects, it always takes the shape of the container that hold it. At a very early age, we begin to discover the properties and behavior of water.

Other concepts we learn through early touch are various textures: soft, hard, rough, smooth, fluffy, fuzzy, furry, sticky, gooey. Without the sense of touch, we could not understand these words. The opportunity to touch and play with a great variety of objects having diverse textures is very important during early childhood because it facilitates conceptualization and language development.

We learn the concept of temperature, particularly in relation to food, through touch. Often we experience pain or surprise when we first touch something hot or cold. Touching also helps us categorize objects by shape and size: round, square, pointed, thin, fat, big, little, and so forth. Through touch, we also learn the concept of weight: heavy, light. Rolling a ball, running a finger around the corner of a cube, trying to lift a heavy rock—these experiences teach us more than a thousand words could convey. As we experience the "feel" of the world's many objects, we "collect" words to describe how they feel when we touch them.

We also begin to develop preferences through touch. We discover that there are some things we like and some we don't like. Given a multitude of opportunities to hold and cherish many toys and objects, we learn to distinguish and show preference for those that are most attractive to us. The identification of these likes and dislikes helps us to express a unique personality.

Tactile perception is a significant sensory experience for the learning child. As children, we learn in a very natural way, through touch, many characteristics of ourselves and the world around us; we then learn to abstract specific characteristics and to categorize them under concepts that we symbolize by words. The more rich and varied our experiences, the greater advantage we have in developing our potential for conceptualization and language acquisition.

## The Meaning of Interpersonal
## Touches in Socialization

During our first eighteen months, we learn the meanings of certain touches in interpersonal relationships and carry these meanings throughout our lives. Certain touches are meant to restrain us, other to delight us. Some are signs of friendship, others of aggression. For example, our mother's grasp around the wrist tells us that our behavior is unacceptable. Throughout life, we recognize this cue without need of supportive verbal communication (Preston 1973). Aging regressed patients who have lost their capability for verbal communication have also been known to understand the meaning of this restraining touch and to respond accordingly.

We also learn that certain touches are designed to tickle us or make us laugh. In our first few months, we remained impervious to such teasing touches, undoubtedly because we were unable to distinguish the separateness of the tickler—an element essential to the success of the exchange. (Note: Efforts to tickle oneself don't work.) Later we are receptive to the fun of tickles. Tickling becomes one of our first social interchanges. Once we learn of the joy, fun, and laughter it causes, we continue to seek out occasions to be tickled, particularly with those we have learned to trust.

Pleasant tickling interchanges increase our potential for more effective sociability before we are able to socialize through speech. They are one-on-one transactions in a shared, caring, tactual communication that allow us to interact with the personality and feeling of those significant persons in our lives.

Beginning as early as the fourth month, we enjoy making contact with our own image in a mirror. Our reflection excites us to use our motor skills to reach out and socialize with the baby in the mirror. Gestures even approach a kind of flirtation as we touch the hands and face of our darling reflected friend. Interest in interacting with the baby in the mirror is carried well beyond the fourth month and appears to be an aid in the healthy development of sociability.

In our developmental years we easily learn the meanings of interpersonal touches. Once we learn them, we use them almost without hesitation. We touch our playmates in friendship. We learn to touch others to express playfulness and to communicate affection. We show leadership by guiding others with a shoulder embrace or by pulling our playmates. As children, we learn to apply symbols to touchings for even the simplest exchanges. We pat others to attract their attention or to give them a greeting. This is later replaced with verbal expressions like "Hi" or "How are you doing?" We stroke stuffed toys, dolls, domestic animals, and younger peers to express love and affection, particularly when we have observed the behavior in our parents or caretakers. Later we learn to verbalize the ideas in expressions like "I like you!" or "I love you." Most of us resort to expressing our aggression and anger with a slap or a punch. It takes us several months, sometimes years, to convert this nonverbal conduct to exclusively verbal expressions like "I don't like you anymore" or "Stop it." Early aggressive contact might include shoving, pushing, or even biting, depending on the severity of the case. Fortunately, with proper guidance, we later learn to symbolize in words these feelings of anger, disgust, and frustration, in order to avoid inflicting physical harm.

# chapter four

# Taboos about Touching: Tracking Them Down

Cultural factors in American society have led us to believe and act as if touching may occur only in intimate and extremely personal relations. We touch for sexual purposes once we have established the ground rules and will occasionally touch to tease, comfort, or hurt others. Without noteworthy exception, however, we have earned the undistinguished title of "the touchless society." We are unable to distinguish between sense awareness and sexual awareness. We need to regain our freedom to touch or not to touch and to become fully prepared to accept the responsibility of touching.

Whom can we touch? When can we touch? What parts of the body can we touch and for how long? Answers to these questions are not easy. They are shrouded by taboos. According to Webster, a taboo is a prohibition imposed by social custom or as a protective measure. In the case of touching taboos, both social custom and protective measures come into play. Taboos have alienated us from our own bodies and taken away a naturalness of human expression. We are "out of touch" with our bodies and stymied in relating to others.

We have the capability to resist taboos and even to eliminate some. To accomplish this, we must first review how we allowed ourselves to become the victims of the touching-taboo traps. We must take stock of the more or less subconscious rules we follow and see if they serve us well. We must question the rationale of what is acceptable and what is not acceptable in touching-behavior patterns handed down to us by our parents and thrust upon us by our peers.

As a first step in gaining a new perspective on your personal touching behavior, take time to write down what you consider acceptable versus unacceptable touching behavior, using the categories on the following chart as a guide. List all the "rules" and "principles" that govern your touching behavior. You may even wish to share your list with your mate or a friend and to exchange ideas. As you proceed through later chapters of *Let's Touch*, consider modifying your list so that it reflects any new touching behaviors you wish to incorporate into your life.

### Personal Rules on Touching

| *Whom* | *When* | *What Part of the Body* | *How* | *How Long* |
|---|---|---|---|---|
| Self | | | | |
| Children | | | | |
| Aged | | | | |
| Mate | | | | |
| Relatives | | | | |
| Close Friends | | | | |
| Acquaintances | | | | |
| Strangers | | | | |

As you continue reading this chapter, compare the taboos it describes to your own concept of acceptable/unacceptable touching behavior. Obviously, there are no right or wrong answers on "to touch or not to touch." We all must choose the touching patterns we wish to follow as individuals. A clear understanding of ourselves and the issues can get us on our way.

## Self-Touching

What about ourselves and our own bodies? Do we feel comfortable about touching ourselves, all the parts of the body? Most of us do not. To some degree, we are hesitant in touching some of our body parts. That is, we tend to refrain from touching parts of the body that have been placed on the taboo list. In effect, we have become strangers to many parts of our very own bodies.

Highest on the taboo list are our genitals. From early childhood we have been told not to touch, explore, or investigate the genital area. Our peers and even some of our parents have passed along a folklore threat. If you play with yourself (they were actually referring to playing with your genitals), you will go blind or crazy. Fortunately, most of us have not heeded the folklore alarm that tried to badger us into refraining from the experience of self-touching. A true story illustrates the desire we have to explore and touch our genitals. A mid-Western youngster was "caught" by his mother while he was "self-exploring." She reprimanded him with the threat of going blind if he continued to do such a thing. Ensnared by how good it felt, he ventured to ask: "Well, can I do it just until I have to wear glasses?"

Why have we had taboos against touching our own genitals? There are perhaps many reasons. Validation of the reasons is still pending. You be the judge. Around the turn of the century, mental hospital patients were "caught in the act" of masturbating; from this observation, several physicians concluded that if mental patients masturbated, then masturbation might be the cause of their illness.

Codes in religions have placed a taboo on masturbation. "Self-abuse" or "self-pleasing" come to be prohibited with the support of biblical interpretation. The story of Onan, son of Judah (Gen. 38:9), is the traditional source. He reportedly spilled his sperm on the ground by deliberately interrupting coitus or by masturbating to prevent insemination of his brother's widow. By not helping to produce an heir, as was his charge under the Hebrew code, Onan himself became the heir to his brother's estate, leaving the widow in poverty. According to more recent scriptural studies, the story was not intended to discourage masturbation, as many earlier interpretations suggested, but to direct attention to the selfish, unjust character of Onan (Kosnik et al. 1977).

Only through the findings of psychologists and researchers of the past thirty years have we come to know that masturbation is a natural human act of self-touching. Over 90 percent of all people engage in masturbation at some time during their lives. There is very little evidence to suggest that self-touching of the genitals may be physically or psychologically harmful. There is a great deal of evidence to suggest that self-touching through masturbation can be beneficial. It has the potential for teaching us the foundations of our sensitivity in sexual relations. It also may benefit us physiologically by releasing sexual tension.

Why should we accept or place severe restrictions on touching our own bodies? The more fully aware we are of the body, the more fully we will be able to accept it. Acceptance of the body can bring us greater acceptance of the self. To become fully aware of the body, we must know what it feels like, what its physical limits are, what its reactions to touching and being touched are. A thorough touching examination of one's own body from head to toe might well become a periodic aspect of self-care. Merely looking at the body in a mirror from different angles doesn't suffice. When we touch the body with our fingers and hands, we experience a more comprehensive reality of it. The touch is firm and reassuring evidence of the body texture, the body lines, and the body limitations. By touching the body on many of its surfaces, crevices, and contours, we lay the foundation for fully knowing the self. This greater awareness will offer us a strengthening closeness to the self and may decrease our dependence on cosmetics and other means of hiding or disguising the body.

Being touchable is what our bodies distinctively have to offer us. There appears to be no need to place a taboo on the act of touching the body when the act is a natural and wholesome expression. Unfortunately, natural acts have not always been viewed as "nice." According to some moral codes, self-touching is contrary to visions of something cleaner and purer for humanity. However, we should consider touching ourselves neither base nor elevating—simply natural.

Equally high on the list of self-touching taboos is the anus. In youth we are taught by implication or direct instruction that we should refrain from touching this area of the body for an obvious reason: it is the final passageway for elimination. We are encouraged to touch the anus only to clean the outside walls, usually done with paper tissue or a cloth. However, we generally have little guidance or instruction on touching the anus to aid us in determining the physical well-being of this vital body part. The taboo on touching this area, though well founded for preventing the spread of germs and disease, has hampered our early detection, through touch, of any physical irregularities.

Similarly to masturbation, self-touching of the breasts has been restricted, for male and female, because of the taboo on seeking self-pleasure. Self-pleasure through touching the breasts is highly unlikely to cause adverse effects. According to many sex psychologists, self-touching to determine the mode and pressure of touch that create the greatest sexual arousal has a high potential for improving sexual self-awareness. Once a woman is able to determine the "right place" and the "right touch" on her breasts—that is, what gives her the most sexual pleasure—she can share that knowledge with a loving mate who can learn to excite her intensely.

Touching the insides of the mouth, the lips, or the nasal

passages in public is taboo for most members of our culture because it is considered uncouth. As young children, we are often reprimanded for "sucking our thumb." We are told either through hearsay or folklore that sucking one's thumb will damage the teeth, cause the mouth to grow in an ugly circle, or misform the lips. Indications from psychologists, dentist, and physicians reporting on child development suggest that we don't have as much to worry about as was once believed. Thumb sucking in moderation is one way for children to comfort themselves. The child who sucks a thumb or a pacifier is able to soothe some of the pain of cutting teeth without harmful after effects.

## Touching Children

The person-to-person contact with the fewest taboos is the touching of infants and children. Our culture seems to permit just about everybody to touch children. Politicians kiss babies. Older brothers and sisters touch the tiny hands and cheeks of the new baby in the family. Neighbors and friends are given unwritten permission to hold, kiss, or caress infants and small children. Perhaps touching infants and young children has not been placed on the list of touching taboos because infants and children, without fully developed verbal skills, are dependent upon tactual expressions for communicating. Most adults are fascinated by tactual communication with infants, as it gives us a chance to share their early life experience, their time of innocence, their freedom to touch and be touched.

Touching taboos begin to invade parent–child relationships at an early age. Yet growing children have a natural need and desire to be touched as a means of being recognized. One way or another, they will seek out physical contact. They will even be disruptive for the "recognition" of a spanking; in some cases, a child learns to associate the pain of a spanking with the pleasure of being recognized. Aptly stated by Burton and Heller (1964):

"What should be pain and avoided becomes pleasure and desired because of the desperate need for human contact. Thus pain becomes exquisite and often the only tangible proof that the person exists." Ironically, as their children mature, some parents fear touching them. They withhold hugs and kisses, and some even withhold spankings, out of a reluctance to touch their children's bodies.

After puberty, our freedom to touch shrinks rapidly. We fall heir to the taboo traps of adulthood. It is a time of groping and uneasiness; we feel bewildered by the many changes happening inside. We and our parents both feel awkward about our new sexual identity. We are impressionable, and the attitudes we pick up about touching may stay with us for many years, maybe for the rest of our lives. The very lack of open communication on touching activities that relate to the sex act can lead us to believe that touching is unacceptable.

Apparently, the onset of adulthood takes away our freedom and innocence and trains us to touch primarily with sexual intentions. Also, the touching range of our own bodies is limited. Society seems to suggest that we cannot tactually explore our bodies as we become adults because, we are told, "You are too old to go around touching yourself," as if the body were not ours to appreciate. In the development of self-touching, we are in great need of modifying our perception. In an enlightened society, we should be able to carry the sense experiences and tactile skills of childhood into adulthood, where they can continue to enrich our lives.

## Touching the Aged

In the helping professions, and even among nonprofessional individuals, there is a resistance to touching or coming into contact with aging persons, as it calls to mind our own mortality. Touching the aged tends to rest on the border of taboo territory, because it forces us to view the destiny of our bodies. The aged, the infirm—especially if we come into contact with them by touching and caring for them—are reminders that we too will lose our youth; we will eventually experience the deterioration of the body. The reminder is disquieting; it contradicts the hidden expectancy—"that will never happen to me."

Perhaps this fear of mortality lies behind our cult of youth. We do not like to touch things that will not feel smooth and taut, that will not enhance our contact with things that are young. The wrinkled skin, gnarled joints, and sometimes swollen hands of the aged turn us off. We seem to fear touching what our culture says is unattractive, as though it could hurt us in some way. Unfortunately, these feelings cause us to limit our touching of the aged to those actions required for their care or guidance—for example, to prevent falls—and perhaps a perfunctory kiss or pat as a greeting or departing gesture. Small children do not share our hang-ups, and they enjoy the cuddling, hand-holding, and caresses of older persons. The aged welcome these loving touches because they, too, as all of us, need to be touched for recognition, understanding, affection, and companionship.

## Touching One's Mate

There are some taboos that influence our behavior in touching our mates. When we are teenagers, we are told not to touch opposite-sex friends sexually. In many families, mothers and fathers exercise a taboo against touching each other in front of their children. They are concerned that the children will not understand their intimate touching behavior. Some parents even provide an atmosphere of nontouching by using twin beds.

Sexual touching of mates is strictly limited in time and place. Some people hesitate to allow their mates to touch them for almost any purpose in public, lest the touch be viewed by others as a sexual stroke. They feel that touching is an exclusively sexual form of encounter and insist upon restricting it to private quarters. This taboo in turn limits touching exchanges for expressing endearment, caring, and warm recognition of one's mate except in certain "approved" public areas like bus depots, train stations, and airports. A comparative study by S.M. Jourard (1966) points out how restrained we are. Opposite-sex couples in other countries don't seem to have the strong taboo on touching partners in public as we seen to have. Jourard observed couples in restaurants and cafes in some of the major cities throughout the world. He reports that couples in London did not touch each other even once during the course of an hour. In Gainesville, Florida, couples touched each other twice during an hour. By comparison, couples in Paris touched 110 times. In the city with the fewest taboos on touching in public, San Juan, Puerto Rico, couples were observed touching each other up to 180 times in the course of an hour.

The trend in touching opposite-sex friends is changing. A comparison of studies conducted in 1966 and 1976 shows that males and females are becoming more open to touching by opposite-sex friends in public (Knapp 1978). Even the areas it is permissible to touch have expanded to body parts previously considered more intimate. So instead of touching only arms, hands, and shoulders in public, we now seem able to touch the thighs, hips, stomach, and even the chest of our opposite-sex friends without challenging the taboos too much.

There are also some taboos associated with touch between mates in private. Some men and women have a taboo on touching opposite-sex partners with their tongues during an embrace. The taboo exists primarily as a result of early childhood training that prohibited using the tongue as a tactual sense organ. Our mothers and fathers restrained us from and admonished us for sticking our tongue out for any purpose; sticking the tongue out was taboo. In adulthood, sticking the tongue out, particularly to touch the tongue of an opposite-sex mate, evokes distaste for some of us. Many of us have broken down our reservations regarding this lovemaking gesture, because we have discovered the erotic sensation it can create.

A taboo on genital-oral contact has permeated relations with opposite-sex partners. Some religious codes have placed restraints on genital-oral contact because the contact, in itself, does not result in procreation. The same rationale would support the taboo against anal intercourse. The fear of harmful bacteria in the genital area, particularly around the urethra and the anus, is another concern with regard to oral-genital contact, so that very few people engage in anal intercourse.

Cuddling in a parent-infant mode is sometimes tabooed between opposite-sex partners. Males, even though they may wish to be cuddled, resist being cuddled and held in an affectionate way, particularly in public, as they feel their masculinity may be put in question. We have permitted the continuation of cultural patterns that view being cuddled as a dependent role, and most males in our society do not wish to be identified as dependency oriented, particularly if it is suggested that they are depending on a female. Women in our society tend to be more open to being cuddled for the sake of cuddling. For the most part, they are not "hung up" on dependency-oriented behavior and tend to seek out cuddling experiences. In many women, however, the desire to be cuddled is camouflaged by a desire to participate in sex for the sake of being cuddled; indeed, they may not be interested in coitus, only cuddling (Hollender 1970). Hopefully, we can learn to perceive cuddling in a different light, one that would not be threatening to men or require women to exchange sex for the comfort and security of being cuddled.

## Touching Relatives

Touching taboos restrict interactions with our relatives. When we greet or take leave of relatives, hugging and touching activities are carefully controlled. As we hug good-bye or hello, we tend to avoid contacts that include the genitals or the breasts. Thus a full frontal body hug with a relative is not common. Most relatives, if they exchange tactual expressions at all, shake hands or give a sideways hug. This type of hug is a side-to-side embrace with one's arm around the waist or shoulder of the other person. Some relatives give cheek kisses or a light shoulder-to-shoulder embrace, making sure that neither breasts nor genitals come into contact. The taboo limiting touching between relatives is most probably rooted in the societal taboo on incest. The potential of the offspring of such unions to be subject to hereditary defects has been a big factor in perpetuating the taboo.

## Touching Close Friends

How do we use touch with a close friend in a nonsexual way? We have taboos on touching friends except under *certain* limited conditions. We are generally limited to a handshake, pats on the back, and an occasional embrace to say hello or good-bye. The same cultural factors prevent us from embracing others (of either sex) to give recognition or understanding or to convey profound friendship. Our culture looks upon even a brief embrace as possibly an intimate or sexual act. Our sense experiences are highly associated with sexuality, mostly attributable to the touch component. The simultaneous upswing in sense communication and sex awareness in our society today frequently makes it difficult to distinguish between the two. The trap of sexual conditioning frequently proves too tenacious for fostering friendly intentions between most men and women (Dancoff 1975). The fear of intimacy itself, in the sense of interpersonal closeness or self-disclosure, is no less a deterrent for many of us. Thus, men and women miss out on many chances for sharing when such an expression of friendship as a hug is called for; the desire to hug is stifled by a long-ingrained taboo.

Even in the case of relating to our closest friends, many of us have a taboo against expressing our deepest feelings of empathy through touch. This constraint seems to originate in our fear of sexual implications and/or our concern that the gesture may place the recipient in a subordinate position or dependency role.

## Touching Acquaintances and Strangers

The taboos that limit our touching exchanges with friends are even more pronounced in our dealings with acquaintances and strangers; we become even more restrictive. The less we know a person, the less likely we are to trust their touches. When someone touches us, it is hard to know his or her intentions. Is it a sexual gesture or a friendly one? We fear mistaking one motive for another.

Although it is a socially acceptable gesture, some people even shy away from a handshake. Have you not found yourself on one side or the other of a handshake in which one party is a reluctant participant? How many of us have held back from offering a handshake because we didn't want to "come on too strong"? The admonition internalized in childhood, "Stay away from strangers," is transformed into not touching them and stays with many of us in adulthood.

In the helping professions, particularly for nurses, there is a definite taboo that calls for systematically refraining from touching or even looking at the genitals of patients. This taboo is founded on the fear that touching the genitals may be misinterpreted. Professionals might even be accused of breaking the ethical code that restricts touching to strictly clinical purposes.

From personal experience as a hospital orderly in my youth, I can attest to the strictness of this code. It was my responsibility to "prep" (shave the body hair) male patients who were scheduled for operations below the waist. I always made a specific point of having the nurse go into the room and explain to the patients beforehand that prepping would be necessary and that an orderly would arrive with a shaving kit. The patients had an absolutely clear understanding of why a member of the hospital staff would be touching them in the genital area. On one occasion, though, when I assumed that the patient's mental "prepping" had occurred, I was wrong. I entered the patient's room, as usual, with my shaving kit in hand, but this time I was greeted with the hostile

51

oath: "Nobody in this hospital is going to touch me on my private parts." Finally, after the nurse explained the need for the procedures the patient allowed me to do the job—but only with his wife nearby as an observer.

Other taboos in the helping professions include touching the patient's head, especially that of an opposite-sex patient, and touching the patient's mouth, except to administer medicine (Watson 1975). There is a strong tendency among patients to view touching these areas as sexual gestures, so nurses generally refrain from such touches unless they are absolutely necessary.

## Where Do We Go from Here?

Taboos on touching will always be with us. There will always be a certain amount of validity to some of them. Awareness of the role they play in our behavior and understanding the reasons behind them can help each of us decide which of these unwritten societal rules we wish to follow.

# chapter five

# Touching for
# Self-Awareness

Awareness of our own bodies as well as our personalities should be one of our life goals. It is through knowing ourselves that we can gain more confidence and trust in ourselves. Through self-awareness we will have the opportunity to become more comfortable with who we are and what we are able to do; from this knowledge, we will be able to manage our own lives better and to attain our goals.

From our perspective here, self-awareness includes knowledge of ourselves, of how others perceive us, and of how we interact with things and people. Touching is a valuable means for gaining self-awareness. As we touch ourselves, we learn more about what our bodies feel like and how we react to our own touches. We can then compare the feeling of our own touches to how we feel upon receiving touches from others. Touching "things" or having "things" touch us also affects the way we feel, even influences the way we behave. Self-awareness through touching and being touched is a significant determinant of personality.

How aware are we of ourselves? Do we know enough about our bodies and personalities to understand ourselves fully and possibly even like ourselves more? Do we know how we react to self-touching, how we feel when others touch us, what we like or dislike when we touch other people or things? What is the effect of touching the clothes we wear, the place where we sit or stand, or the bed we lie in at night? All of these touchings, sometimes consciously and sometimes unconsciously, influence our state of mind. Everything we touch has an impact, however small, on the way we feel about ourselves, the way we view our world, and the way we react to the environment. An anecdote may illustrate the effect of the things that touch us and how we have insulated ourselves from the sense of touch. A conservative businessman, always formally dressed in a starched shirt, coat, and tie, had the feeling that he was going to die; he was having trouble breathing and felt anxious and confined but had no idea as to the possible cause of his dis-ease. After consulting his doctor, he found his problem less serious then he had anticipated. The doctor observed that the businessman's collar was two sizes too small, cutting off circulation and reducing his ability to breathe. In this extreme case, then, awareness of the clothes that were touching, even "strangling," him became critically significant. Needless to say, he thereafter proceeded to wear the right size clothes and became completely cured.

## Achieving Self-Awareness Through Self-Touch

The findings of body awareness groups indicate that we are only vaguely conscious of our bodies—their size, shape, and reaction to touch. Evidently, we have not let our bodies "feel" to their fullest potential. We have insulated them from our very selves. As a result, we neither fully understand nor enjoy our physical selves.

As infants and young children, we spent great amounts of time investigating our own bodies, visually and tactually. During infancy, we closely examined our feet and toes, swatted at them, and grabbed hold of them; we even tried to put them in our mouths. During our early years, we "played doctor" and examined our bodies (and those of our friends), inserting an exploring finger into crevices and openings, pressing here and there to see how it would feel. Some of us were "caught" in our touching games and, unfortunately, may have been reprimanded or told it was "not nice." How many of us, though, have ever consciously touched and explored the openings, crevices, rims, and textures of our bodies in adulthood? It is only through healthy self-touching that we can become fully aware of the body, with complete physical awareness of the self. The absence of touching is compensated for by other behaviors, which in extreme cases are characteristic of neuroticism and mental disorders. We are our bodies. We "owe" them, and they are ours to care for and enjoy. A thorough examination of the body, repeated periodically, can help us know the wonder of ourselves. It can also help us detect serious health problems in their early stages.

*Genital Self-Touching for Awareness of the Sexual Self.* Many people have failed to seek out the great benefits of self-touching the genital area for a better understanding and appreciation of the sexual self. The taboo against genital self-touching and masturbation has deeply affected many of us—so much so that we either restrict ourselves from such self-touching altogether or feel ashamed or guilty if we do "indulge." Despite this long-ingrained taboo, most of us experience our first orgasms through self-touching and self-arousal. Such self-touching is extremely valuable in developing an awareness and love of oneself, which is essential to the ability to love another person sexually.

In addition to creating a comfortable self-acceptance, self-touch teaches a person about his or her own sensitive areas and sexual responses. Communicating this self-knowledge to a partner plays a vital role in achieving a pleasurable sexual relationship. Just as learners are responsible for their own learning, so we are responsible for our own sexual pleasure. Our dependence on another person for sexual pleasure cannot be absolute. If we do not know our own potential for sexual response very well, we cannot expect a partner magically to know how to satisfy us. Being able to tell a partner the locations, modes, and rhythms of touch we enjoy will help us achieve sexual fulfillment.

Some people learn to explore their bodies and masturbate for the first time as part of sex therapy. In recent years, sex therapists have found that such self-exploration, when reflected upon and shared with one's partner, has tremendous potential for helping couples to improve their sexual experience. Because many women traditionally have been quite inhibited about genital self-touching, therapists have found it beneficial to conduct seminars in which a group of women support and learn from one another in a wholesome approach to this new behavior; the group sessions typically involve a sharing among members of feelings about their bodies and a discussion of gradual steps in exploring their sexual selves.

How can we learn about our personal sensitive spots? We can simply seek them out by exploring the entire body. The breasts, whether male or female, and the genitals are generally the most sensitive. Each area, though, will respond differently, depending on the individual and the type of stroke.

For the female, there are two specific areas that, when touched appropriately, assist in producing the delightful sensations experienced in orgasm. The first such area is the clitoris. It is located on a shaft in the upper portion of the vulva and is protected by a clitoral hood. The vaginal walls do not always provide a natural lubrication to the clitoral hood or shaft. Touching and stroking the clitoris can be uncomfortable if contact is made without the application of natural fluids from inside the vagina or a sterile lubricant.

The second area very important in female orgasm is a muscle located about an inch to an inch and a half up on the inside of the vaginal canal. Technically referred to as the pubococcygeus muscle, and commonly called the PC muscle, it can provide a woman with great pleasure when it is drawn tight and stimulated with the fingers or an erect penis. Deliberately tightening and releasing this muscle can be pleasurable and can enhance the response to stimulation. Exercising the PC muscle is recommended, particularly for women whose PC muscle is weak. Strengthening this muscle can lead to more pronounced contractions of the vagina and greater pleasure during orgasm (Zastrow and Chang 1977).

Women can benefit greatly from exploring the clitoris and the area around the PC muscle to determine which modes of touch and specific combinations of touch feel best, producing a tingling sensation and enlargement (or erection) of the clitoris. It is best not to limit touches exclusively to the clitoral area. If a woman can stimulate the area around the opening of the vaginal canal and rhythmically tighten the PC muscle at the same time the clitoris is stimulated, she will be able to experience a sensation that can lead to a very intense orgasm. To many women, this experience is much more satisfying than simple touches to the clitoris, which tend to evoke less intense orgasms.

There is more to creating an orgasm than touching the clitoris and the PC muscle. One must be able to create a relaxing mood and envision sexually exciting fantasies. All of these, plus the touching, contribute to a mind set that allows the pleasure-flowing feeling of an orgasm to occur.

Women can experience their first orgasms alone, as they respond to their own touches and caresses. A loving partner in the first experience may be a distraction from exploring one's own body. Once a woman learns about all her body sensations, which areas are least and most pleasure giving, she will be able to explain and share these secrets with her mate. Most truly loving experiences are a result of sharing. And what greater sharing can we offer to a trusted loved one than the knowledge of the most pleasurable and sensitive parts of our bodies?

Most men experience their first orgasm without a mate. Through self-touching and seeking out sensitive areas of the body, men learn to produce erections of the penis and attain the acme of sexual tension, which is released in orgasm. They can share the intimate knowledge of their preferences in genital touching with their sexual partner.

Men's self-touching can teach lessons just as valuable as women's. One such lesson centers on the expectancy of penile erections. Males learn that prolonged self-touching will not always bring a continuous erection. Just as vaginal lubrication and dilation are subject to peak periods for the female, penile erection is subject to peak periods for the male. Through self-exploration, men can learn that an erection may subside without ejaculation and recur again shortly; this can happen several times before a climax is reached. Men can then relax with this knowledge as they seek their own enjoyment and that of their loving partner.

Through exploration, men can also learn to recognize the sensations that immediately precede ejaculation. Such knowledge can help them learn to control the time of ejaculation, particularly if they wish to prolong an erection in coitus to better satisfy their mate. Such self-knowledge is not only useful in a sexual encounter but gives the man a greater sense of confidence in his sexual ability. A relaxed atmosphere, physical well-being, and freedom from anxiety are also necessary for men to enjoy a sexual experience fully.

## Self-Awareness Through Touching Things

Idiomatic expressions in everyday language suggest a perspective on touching as it relates to self-awareness. If we hear of individuals with their "heads in the clouds," we can imagine several things about them. They are "up in the air" and are not able to see things, because they "don't have their feet on the ground." Underlying these expressions is the assumption that the most reasonable perspective on ourselves, reality, and other persons is obtained when we have our feet securely touching the ground. In reality, there is a lot of truth to the idea. We are in constant touch with the ground, the floor, or the earth. We touch the chairs we sit in, we touch the ground as we move from one place to another. The whole body touches the bed where we sleep. This constant touch with the earth and things of the earth produces an unconscious sense of security. We take these touches for granted. However, if they are not there when we expect them to be, we can lose our sense of stability. A traumatic example may occur when we walk along a dark street at night, expecting to touch the "flat earth" with every step; we may reach a point where one foot does not touch the ground as anticipated because there is a pothole where we expected secure footing. Immediately, our stability is threatened. What we took for granted suddenly was not there. We lost touch with our stable referent and consequently lost our orientation to the rest of the world. We may have twisted an ankle and possibly lost our self-confidence when walking in the street on dark nights. As with many other benefits of touch, we only realize the significance of firm footing when we lose it.

In infancy and early childhood we were prolific touchers. We touched everything within reach. The desire to touch more things motivated us to crawl and walk. Touching those things that attracted our attention helped us to form our first feelings about things we liked and things we didn't like. We formed our concepts via the things we touch. At one point in early development, we began to conceive that we were separate from the things we touched. For our first few months, we were unable to distinguish where our bodies ended and other things began. Once we were able to touch a block, hold it in our hands, and throw it away, we were on our way to learning which things were part of us. Conversely, when we grabbed a foot with our hands, tried to throw it away, and, with great puzzlement, found that it could not be thrown too far and that it kept coming back, we became aware that the foot was a part of us.

As we continued to develop in the first year of life, we cultivated our preference for things through the sense of touch. Certain objects attracted our attention and held our interest because of the way they felt. If an object like a blanket or a doll felt soft and we felt comfortable touching it, we became aware of a texture that pleased us. We discovered that we liked smooth, soft, or silky objects. We became more aware of our touch preferences. As young children, most of us also discovered that we liked to touch round objects like balls and marbles. Most of us did not cultivate a liking for sharp or pointed objects, for obvious reasons. Our early reality, for the most part, was gained through things we touched and our responses to them. The way we "felt" about them constituted our awareness of personal preferences.

As teenagers or adults most of us become very unhappy when we are treated as if we have no real identity. Our world has become impersonalized, with its overcrowded cities, overcrowded universities, and overcrowded freeways, each packed with unidentified masses of people. It is difficult to find the "real me" in the masses. We are a license number on a car. We are an identification number at the university and a census number in the cities. Even in hospitals, we are impersonally identified as "the case in room 324" or "the appendectomy in room 515."

It is little wonder that adolescents are in search of greater self-awareness for clarifying who they are. Their search for self and self-awareness leads them to touch more things, try out new life-styles, new behaviors, new experiences—trying to know the full self under as many variations in stimulation as are humanly possible. They test new hairstyles, new clothes or methods of dress, new handshakes, new methods of dancing—touching or nontouching in every way imaginable—to see if "it is me!" They are highly motivated to find the "real me," and when they do, they feel more comfortable with themselves.

## Self-Awareness Through Touching
## Exchanges with Others

We depend greatly upon our interactions with others for information about who we are and what our physical and mental boundaries are. Beginning in infancy, we judge ourselves, become aware of ourselves, by the way we think others "see" us. The more we value people, the more we value the way we think they see us. Our parents have a great impact on our self-awareness, because it is through their eyes that we begin to visualize ourselves. We look to our parents first to learn who and what we are. They mirror the "self" back to us, and what we see in that mirror is the primary image we hold of ourselves.

When parents demonstrate their love by physically touching and caressing us, we see ourselves as deserving of their love. If we are neglected and deprived of those touching activities that communicate love and caring, we will begin to think of ourselves as unlovable. Infants are not objective. We tend to accept loving touches or the lack of them as a valid indication of our identity: a lovable or unlovable person. We begin to internalize: "If my mother and father touch me in loving ways, then I must deserve such treatment." We feel that we are "worthy" persons, and we learn to like ourselves. At a very young age, we are unable to understand our parents' actions fully. We cannot say to ourselves: "I know and understand my parents. They are too busy to give me loving touches." In our naiveté, we are more apt to feel: "My parents do not come close to me; they do not touch me as a means of expressing love for me. Therefore, I am not worthy of their touches; I am not worthy of their love." By the time we are mature enough to evaluate ourselves with reasonable objectivity, our awareness of self and our self-concept are set. Our self-perception has determined well-formed behavior patterns. We cannot alter our self-concept thereafter without making a considerable effort.

To complicate matters, those of us who feel "unacceptable" because of a lack of loving touches frequently behave in ways that are distracting to others in order to attract the attention we crave. We may have become so hungry for others to touch us that we will do almost anything to receive those physical "strokes" that communicate endearment: we may refuse to disagree with others or have great difficulty in refusing favors, even when those favors conflict with our values or convenience. When we are severely deprived of tactual experience, we may take extreme measures to gain the experience of being touched. In the absence of contact with others, we begin to touch ourselves. We might touch the more sensitive areas like the mouth, the ears, the nose, and the genitals and, in the process, gain a greater sense of pleasure or displeasure yielded from touching varying parts of the body. Touch deprivation has led some youth into annoying or irrational behavior that they display even though they know it will bring about physical punishment. Negative physical contact replaces positive physical contact as a means of recognition of the self. The need is so strong that the individual feels it is better to be recognized in a negative physical way than not to be recognized at all. It is emotionally destructive of the self-concept to be totally deprived of any means of becoming physically aware of one's "self." We desperately need touches from others as recognition of our being.

As we move into adolescence, we are constantly interacting with people other than our parents who have an impact on our self-awareness. These significant figures are continually giving us feedback about the way they "see" us or "feel" us. If our interactions with them, verbal and nonverbal, result in our identification as kind, even-tempered, and trustworthy people, we extend our self-awareness to those concepts. Conversely, if these significant others treat us as unkind, ill-tempered, and undeserving of touches for recognition and love, our self-awareness is modified from the earlier concepts, and the parental influence is partially negated.

Teenagers, particularly those of economically and socially

deprived areas in the United States, have expressed their dilemma in the crisis of self-awareness. They are not sure who they are or what they are. Many do not know who they would like to become. They feel anger but are not sure at whom they should direct it. They fear, without knowing fully the source of their fear. They feel rejected but are unable to detect the source. It may very well be that their feelings result from insufficient recognition in their developmental years. The crisis of self-awareness is more severe in minority groups, particularly if these teenagers accept a picture of themselves as uncultured and unlovable. The resolution of the crisis is an important developmental task of late adolescence and early adulthood. Touch, particularly from significant others, has great potential for providing the recognition that is critically necessary at this time.

Research shows that men and women who are touched on the hands, even if they are unconscious of the touches, tend to develop a self-awareness that includes more positive feelings toward themselves (Winter 1976). People who receive warm and friendly touches on the hands seem to receive the message that they are valued by those who touch them; being valued by others, they consequently feel more positive and confident about themselves. Greater self-confidence and self-esteem enable persons to go about their daily lives with greater self-reliance and ease. Such persons seem to manage their lives more effectively.

Trust in ourselves and in others is gained, to a significant degree, through touching experiences. We gain our sense of trust first through our parents' touches, and then through interaction with other significant figures in our lives. These interactions influence our ability to relate to others.

Up to this point, our discussion has included only our passive participation as recipients of touch. Research also shows that active touchers have a greater potential for self-awareness. A high correlation exists between touching and self-disclosure (Lomranz and Shapira 1974). If we exhibit a high level of touching, we also tend to exhibit a high level of self-disclosure.

Touchers tend to talk more about themselves and share more of their feelings with others. Also, those who accept touching tend to be more willing to talk about themselves and communicate more openly with their friends and associates. As we disclose more of ourselves to others, we become more aware of ourselves. Others tend to "bring out" those feelings, those frustrations, those joys and pleasures that perhaps we are incapable of articulating by ourselves. As we reflect with others and are more motivated to do so through touching, we gain a greater self-knowledge. We also tend to judge ourselves by what others think of us. Through interpersonal sharing, what we truly are is revealed to trusted friends and to ourselves.

A study of encounter groups has shown that self-disclosure can be encouraged through touching exchanges (Cooper and Bowles 1973). The purpose of the encounter groups was to improve participants' self-awareness by facilitating self-disclosure. In those groups where touching exercises were employed, there was a greater degree of self-disclosure. Encounter groups involving touching exercises, though, are not a panacea for improving self-awareness. Another experiment has shown that most people are uneasy about such touching exercises and find such a situation stressful (Walker 1975).

If we are not inclined to get involved in an encounter group but wish to make use of touching exchanges to break down barriers and facilitate self-disclosure, what can we do? Initially, we should recognize and respect our natural inclinations and those of the people with whom we wish to relate. Men are particularly disinclined to touching exchanges with other men, most probably because of a fear of homosexual implications. This explains the apparent contradiction in the fact that our highest degree of self-disclosure occurs with same-sex friends, whereas our highest level of touching behavior occurs with opposite-sex friends. The least amount of self-disclosure occurs between individuals and their parents, particularly in the father–son relationship (Lomranz and Shapira 1974). Bearing these generalizations in mind, we can begin by observing our present modes of interaction with others. We determine if our present verbal interaction is accompanied and supported by meaningful touching. If touching interchanges are included, we may wish to determine their extent and see if verbal communications increase or decrease with supportive touching exchange. For example, if a loved one or friend is reserved about expressing ideas, we might help that individual to disclose them more freely if we touch him or her with an encouraging pat on the shoulder. Chances are, if the person is not overly shy, he or she will respond positively to the touch and will feel more able to express those ideas. The verbal and tactual sharing will have a corresponding positive effect on us. We open up more and are willing to express more with those we trust. Touching creates a confidence that permits us to articulate our innermost feelings more easily.

# chapter six

# Touching for Communication

## Nonverbal Communication

In spite of its lack of universal acceptance and relative consistency in meaning, touching is the most meaningful form of nonverbal communication. There is much evidence in the research literature to confirm this. But let's see if we can compare some examples of visual communication with touching communication to decide for ourselves. Let's say we wish to communicate that we love someone; he or she will receive our message either via touch or visually, by observing our body motion. We stand with a caring expression and open arms as a cue to express love. The message is observed by the intended receiver. We then take the same open arms and place them around the receiver. Chances are good that the touching message has the most meaning for that person. The message is more likely to be felt than seen.

Let's compare another touching communication with another visual cue. In this case, we wish to communicate an imminent danger to the recipient. We wish to advise a pedestrian to alter his or her course since there is a dangerous obstacle ahead. We provide a visual cue by shaking the head in a negative way, raising the arms, and turning the palms of the hands toward the individual, moving them in a stopping signal. By contrast, to advise the person with a touching communication, we quickly move nearby, grab an arm, and guide the person from danger. If we could measure the meanings of the visual message and the touching message, we would surely find the touch much more direct and, consequently, a more complete and meaningful communication.

A teacher and mother of two children in Long Beach gave an account of the greater meaning conveyed when she used touching as a supportive mode. She made an evaluation of the touching interaction between her twelve-year-old son, her fourteen-year-old daughter, and herself. To her surprise, she found that she had had fewer touching contacts with her children over the preceding six months than in the previous six months, partly because of her preoccupation with a new work assignment. She had relied to a great extent on words when she communicated with her children about their homework and disappointing grades. She also recalled that she had used much visual communication, shaking her head to react to unacceptable behavior. She decided to include more touching communication with her children.

A good opportunity arose when they brought home grades lower than expected. Instead of using a negative verbal approach, she seated the children on the couch with her, one on each side. She placed her arms around them, drawing them close to her body, and began to review the marks. She expressed her disappointment in seeing such low grades for youngsters with "known capabilities." As they huddled together, they agreed on a plan of action. They would review each homework assignment that created difficulty for the children. And when those occasions occurred, the mother made a special effort to be in touching contact with the struggling youngsters.

**67**

The message in the activity was clear in the mother's mind: she was expressing interest and concern. She felt that the meaning of her message was also encouragement: "to see things through during difficult times." She was successful, and she has since reported that there is a direct correlation in her household between hugging and higher grades.

## Touching Communicates Feelings and Attitudes

How do you communicate your feelings or attitudes? Like others, you probably often hesitate to use words, unretractable and glaring as they often are. Instead, you turn to touch.

One type of subtle visual communication of feeling is self-touching. Although we're often unaware of these movements, we send definite messages to those around us. One classic example is Cassandra, an active PTA member in Fresno, California. Chairperson of the social committee, Cassandra always takes responsibility for organizing the biannual fund-raising banquet. As she oversees the final preparations, Cassandra grabs at the pleats of her skirt every five minutes or so, moving them back and forth. Co-workers needn't look at the clock to sense that zero hour is approaching. The pleat adjustment tells them that arrival is imminent. Cassandra's message is more specific in communicating anxiety than if she were to confide, "I sure hope everything will turn out all right."

Another type of self-touch is finger snapping, primarily used to call attention to the self through sound. Several years ago on a road show, a well-known male singer from Los Angeles inadvertently snapped his way out of a communications impasse. The singer was working with a new band that had previously played for a female singer. Very attentive to her mood and movements, the band backed her flawlessly. The transition to a new performer didn't go well. They seemed inattentive, out of sync. In rehearsals, the new singer began to instruct them—slower here, faster there—but to no avail. Finally, he tried to stop the musicians midsong by loudly snapping his fingers. In defiance, the players played on. Angry finger snapping and musical beats were exchanged. The fracas continued for about five minutes, until the band members and singer broke into laughter and then moved into a unified beat guided by the snapping of fingers. A few angry snaps led the band first to awareness and then to communication with the singer.

Communication between sex partners can also be affected by subtle differences in touching techniques. Delia, a restaurant manager in San Francisco, reported her efforts to communicate through touch. On many occasions during the busy season, Delia had to work straight through for twelve or fourteen hours. Naturally, when she arrived home, she was disinclined to have sexual relations with her husband. She would crawl into bed and kiss him gently on both cheeks in a sexually nonaggressive manner. Then she would turn on her side, drawing his arm around her to place his hand just above her waist. This touching was a highly acceptable communication to her husband; she loved him and wanted to be close to him in a nonsexual way. No excuses had to be fabricated, no feelings were hurt.

## Touching Communicates Warmth, Confidence, and Concern

The model for communicating warmth is the mother. She provided the first awareness of warmth as we lived and grew inside her body. We seek unconsciously and consciously to reidentify and reexperience that primal warmth. From our earliest years, we associated warmth with parental contacts. When we felt cold, we sought out and snuggled up to the warm, mature bodies of our parents; we found great comfort in jumping in bed with them and absorbing their pleasurable warmth. We continue throughout our lives to be attracted to and to long for the warmth that can be provided through the act of touching or being touched.

In contrast, most of us can agree that we respond negatively to cold hands on our bare skin. We withdraw from the chilling discomfort. There is a negative connotation to being touched by objects that are cold. Our aversion to cold is reflected extensively throughout the language. We have expressions like "He is a cold-hearted person," "They gave her the cold shoulder," and "At the last minute he got cold feet." Similarly, our senses react negatively to extreme heat or hot objects. This negative position is also reflected in the language with expressions like "The job was too hot to handle" and "He is a hot-headed person." Somewhere in between these two extremes is the more widely accepted medium—warm. Of course, physically we prefer it, and psychologically we respond best to it. Warm, as a concept, is more closely related to the temperature of the human body and thus more closely aligned to the temperature to which we are accustomed. We also express this acceptance positively with phrases like "She is a warm person" and "The thought warms my heart." If we use the body's natural warmth and avoid extending either a cold or a hot and sweaty hand, we can communicate the pleasing message of warmth through touching.

Handshaking is commonly the initial mode of communication through touch, and of course, the hand's skin surface reflects the individual's emotional state. The highly sensitive person can determine if the verbal message being sent is congruent with the tactual communication. If the two cues do not match, the entire message may be subject to question.

An example of the significance of tactual communication through handshaking was reported to me by Jason, a highly trained and skilled automotive mechanic. He completed a two-year auto mechanic program in Los Angeles after graduating from Hollywood High School. His vocational counselor worked diligently for several weeks in attempting to locate a job for him. He sent Jason to a dozen or more auto mechanic shops for interviews; none was successful. He could not understand why he had not gotten a job. As a last recourse, his vocational counselor called the last three employers who interviewed Jason. Each employer reported that Jason was able to verbalize his ability to perform the work expected of him effectively; however, all three employers reported that Jason's hands perspired so severely that they doubted either his cleanliness or his self-confidence. Neither impression was positive. Jason has since modified his method of handling stressful situations; his hands are drier, and he has acquired an excellent job.

The helping professions, specifically the fields of medicine and nursing, need practitioners of touching who can communicate maturity. There is a great need for patients to be touched in the right way by nurses and doctors. Among the severest of complaints by patients is that they feel they have been handled roughly by uncaring doctors and nurses. This type of complaint seems to occur more predominately in hospitals served by medical students. In one hospital, I interviewed twenty patients, fourteen of whom reported that the staff looked upon them as statistics rather than as persons who had had the misfortune to contract a disease. Eight of the fourteen patients pointed out that their experiences in being touched by staff members were highly unfavorable; they felt like objects, not people.

Sally, one of the patients interviewed, had a different experience. She had a back injury that left her in severe pain and partially immobile. She had never depended on anyone to help her in moving around. Her condition now called for this help. Wilma, a petite nurse with a Southern accent, was assigned to work with Sally. Wilma surveyed Sally's condition, patiently inquiring about and noting those locations on Sally's body that caused her the most pain. Wilma also carefully asked about and determined, by light touches and cautious movements, which parts of Sally's body could be moved without difficulty. After deliberation of ten or fifteen minutes, Wilma was able to move Sally to desired changes in position, causing only minimal discomfort. Also, Sally was bathed without experiencing severe discomfort. Wilma's touches were confidently and caringly given. They exemplify the touching acts of a mature and warm person. Even when touches serve a pragmatic or clinical purpose, the warmth and care with which they are given are very significant to the recipient. A clinical procedure that is carried out correctly but coldly is just not good enough. Patients are human beings; they are sensitive to tactual communication, be it caring or uncaring.

## A Pat Helps Motivate

One of the most effective means of expressing nurturance is the burping touch given to babies. This act promotes babies' growth and well-being by relieving their discomfort. I believe that this early experience provides the foundation for our general acceptance of pats on the back to communicate nurturance and emotional support. Very few of us have any resistance to receiving "a pat on the back" to tell us we are doing a good job. Generally, we interpret this type of touch as encouragement and approval.

An insurance executive in Anaheim, California, spoke to me about his success in applying touch to a personnel problem. He had hired part-time college students for the monthly filing of clients' record-of-payment cards but found that they soon became bored with the monotonous job. The turnover rate was very high. The executive progressively increased the pay scale in hopes of reducing the turnover rate, but without success. He became seriously concerned about the misfiled cards and the increase in the cost to have them filed. He was in a dilemma. He had used verbal praise with the employees, but that did not seem to improve the situation. Finally, he attended a seminar on interpersonal relationships with office employees and found that several employers had success in using touch to motivate workers. He tried their technique, a light pat on the back with verbal praise, and found that the turnover rate dropped and filing efficiency increased within three months.

## Touching Facilitates Self-Disclosure

A basic feeling of "being distant" or "being close" to other persons is related to our willingness to disclose ourselves to them. If we feel close to other people, we tend to tell more about ourselves than when we feel "distant". A feeling of "being close" is increased when we touch or are touched by another person. As a result, we feel freer to talk about ourselves, our hopes and desires, our concerns and fears. We are less likely to communicate openly with those who are "distant." Their "distance" seems to create a greater risk in our openness with them.

When I worked as a hospital orderly during my teens, I found that those patients who were gently touched, particularly on the forearms, became more ready to talk about themselves than those who resisted being touched. An elderly female cardiac patient resisted communicating with anyone, even her own doctor. One day, as I was fitting an oxygen tent around her, I touched the upper part of her arms with my hands and gently told her that I hoped she could now breathe better. She opened her eyes more fully, gave me a half smile, and said she was pleased to have the tent adjusted. Each afternoon I would return and check her breathing, and each time I touched her on the arms, she became more willing to engage in a few minutes of conversation about herself.

## Appropriateness of Touch

To be effective as a means of communication, touches must be given in an appropriate context and with appropriate intensity. Have you ever observed the messages, ideas, and feelings being

**73**

communicated in a pantomime? The mime artists express their meanings without words by using actions and movements. They are able to "say things" by the way they act; however, their movements are exaggerated. They construct an artificial communication that exaggerates the intended meaning. The results usually communicate comic relief or tragedy. Circus clowns are mime artists. The predominant aspects of their messages are reflected in their madeup faces. Their mouths are drawn in an uncommonly large smile or with long, sad lines. Their eyebrows are exaggerated lines curved over their foreheads. Their clothes are in artificially small or large sizes that add to their comic or tragic appearance. Their communications are visual only, for the most part, and we do not take them seriously, as we expect humor in their performance. When a male clown kisses a female clown, even though the action is intended to project romance, we still see it as a little humorous. When a clown takes the hand of an opposite-sex clown and caresses tenderly, we still see it as part of the humor in a clown's make-believe world. By contrast, when two young lovers in the real world kiss or hold hands in a caring way, the communication is clear, to the lovers and to observers, that their actions are not on a comic level. They are communicating, through their touching activities, a sincere message of tenderness and love. A caress or a kiss given under the wrong circumstances or given too lightly or too intensely may be misunderstood.

Another psychologist reported to me several years ago of a professional clown who could not step out of his "clown character" when it became necessary to communicate about a serious subject in the real world. Pepe came from a family of circus showpeople. He was originally from Spain and had traveled all over the world with his parents. He was an only child, with great admiration for his parents, and he sought to follow in their footsteps in the circus. As a youngster, he earned spending money by feeding the circus animals. He was fascinated with the clowns and hoped someday to be one himself. He started by doing bit parts with an older clown. He learned the routine so well that he eventually became a big-time professional clown. He "lived" being the clown, both onstage and off. When he was twenty-six, he met Cecelia, an elephant trainer. He fell in love with her and tried to express his feelings, but they always came out in the antics of a clown. After several months of practice at not being a clown offstage, Pepe took Cecelia for a walk in the countryside. He refrained from his usual antics. At appropriate times, he touched his lips lightly to hers, repeating this same gesture many times without saying a word. The message was more clearly received than his former visual antics.

Expressive touching, or touching with an extra measure of meaning, is our best means of communicating support and nurturance. A key example of expressive touching is seen on the football fields in this country. Football players express their support of other players' actions by patting them on the buttock with an open, flat hand. It is not uncommon for a player to receive an approving pat or two after completing a crucial pass or making a touchdown. One might ask why the buttock is used for this communication. Among men in football uniforms, the buttock is probably the most accessible place for direct body contact. Patting the buttock, though common among football players on the field, is not commonly used off the field or by players out of uniform. The same type of contact off the field and out of context of the game might be misinterpreted and convey an entirely different meaning.

A well-known quarterback, headed for retirement from a California team, told me his embarrassing experience with the derrière pat. Experiencing a diminishing interest in playing ball, he contacted a realtor to assist him in locating a commercial business that he could purchase and manage. The realtor spent many weeks in search of the right property. Day after day, he studied the new listings, driving out to review the potentials of one piece of property after another. After much searching, the realtor found a fast-foods restaurant that intrigued the two of them.

They inspected the business and observed a heavy noon-hour lunch crowd. Enthusiastic about the profits he imagined, the quarterback excitedly extended his right hand and patted the realtor several times on the fanny, exclaiming, "That's great, that's the kind of business I want"—all in full view of the crowd. Needless to say, the communication, though well intended, gave some cause for concern to the realtor and the onlookers.

## Discomfort in Being Touched

Touching can bring discomfort and negativism to some people. Authorities estimate that 20 percent of all persons in the United States feel some discomfort in touching or being touched. This means that at least one in every five persons we encounter will have a limited aversion to touching activity.

Two percent of our population feels severe discomfort with touching of any kind and cannot accept it under any circumstances. An elderly lady in Chicago evidently was a member of this group. Whenever she walked in the streets, rain or shine, she always carried an umbrella cane with her. On many occasions she had been approached by younger people who wished only to help her cross the street safely. They would take her gently by the arm as she attempted to cross alone, offering to guide and support her. She would immediately tighten her hand around the umbrella cane and begin striking with all her might at the intruder. The same unfortunate set of circumstances would occur even when persons near her own age attempted to help her.

Her resistance to touch and being touched was demonstrated even with close members of her family. One of her daughters spoke of occasions when her mother used the cane as a shield to keep her two grandchildren from coming into contact with her. On no occasion would she allow anyone to touch her, even for services like having her hair cut (she did it herself) or for medical services; she explained to the doctor where the pains were and how they felt in her body. but he was never allowed to touch her in an examination.

Another instance in discomfort with touching is the case of a young Cleveland mother. After delivering her first and only child, she became a nontoucher. She refused to touch her own child directly, as she felt it as "unclean" to do so. She took great pains to avoid any contact with her baby. If no one was around to change the child's diapers for her, she would clean her hands thoroughly, put on a pair of rubber gloves, and then proceed to change the child's diaper "without ever touching the baby." (Fortunately, the father and grandparents of the child demonstrated a more positive attitude and touched and cuddled the child at every opportunity.)

Some members of our society use touching intentionally to release their own frustrations while causing discomfort to others. If you have ridden a subway in New York or in almost any part of the world, you may have observed or experienced this type of touching. During the busy hours on a New York subway, some riders push their way through the crowd, mashing their own bodies against the maze as if the people in it were nonhuman pieces of cardboard. At the rush hour in a London subway, one rider habitually touched the palms of his hand in a spearlike design and charged through the masses, causing considerable discomfort to those unfortunate enough to be in his path.

Males touching females, causing them discomfort in the close quarters of Mexico City's subways, have become a great concern to the subway's management. Evidently, many of the young males riding the subways sought out females, standing close to them. Then they move through the crowd with open hands, touching all reachable females on the breasts or genitals, causing severe discomfort among the women. The situation became so disruptive that the management has modified travel regulations, mandating separate cars for men and women.

Discomfort at being touched, however, is not a dead end for most people. If we know individuals who manifest some uneasiness or reluctance about touching exchanges, we should respect their feelings. We might find them open to a touching gesture if we simply advise them beforehand of our plan to touch them. Also, we may benefit by giving them the reason why we wish to touch them before we actually do so.

An elderly professional man and his middle-aged son were hesitant and felt some discomfort in touching each other beyond the usual handshake. They lived in different cities. The son visited his father once or twice a year. They greeted each other at the airport with a handshake. Also, as they parted, they would clasp hands, and shake them up and down in the standard gesture. The son began reading the literature on touching and touch deprivation after returning home from one of these trips. He decided that on the next visit with his father, he would break the chain of touching resistance. Reflecting on his father's age and the possibility that each visit might easily be the last, the son changed from the handshake routine to a highly communicative message of caring. On the next visit, as he waited for the flight announcement, he decided to change the way he would express his departing message. He called his father close to him and said: "Dad, I'm going to embrace you. I'm doing this to show you that I care, that I think you are a fine person, and that I love you." The two men stood holding each other in a long, tearful embrace.

## Fear of Dependency

As infants, we received many touches from persons who fed, changed, and bathed us. We were dependent upon adults who were both superior to us and larger than we were. Our subtle, infant behavior pattern of accepting or not accepting their touching is the foundation for the touching patterns and feelings about being touched that we have in later life. We pass through the teenage years with an outward disdain for the need to be touched and cared for by our parents, because we think the need shows our dependency upon them. Yet, inwardly, we maintain a longing to be touched in a parental way throughout our lives. It is conceivable that we continue to allow those who are more mature, of higher rank, or with parental qualities to touch us when we are willing to accept the dependency role that is associated with this activity. On the other hand, many persons are unwilling to accept being touched, even by their peers, because it conveys to them a discomforting sense of dependency.

## The Mode Affects the Meaning

In touch communication, the mode of the touch is significant and influences the meaning. A pat on the head, to a small child, is considered a friendly gesture, whereas a light stroke on the head of the same child is considered a loving gesture; in most cases, the act of touching by patting is given and received as a friendly gesture, and the act of touching by stroking is a loving gesture. When a person is open enough to pat the knees of a person of the opposite sex, it is generally given and received as an act of friendliness; this assumes, of course, that the recipient is open enough to accept the gesture. When the knees are stroked in a gentle manner, particularly over a long period of time, the act is clearly a loving or sexually oriented gesture. In either case, the mode of the touch is the factor that determines the meaning.

## Avoiding Misinterpretations of Touch Communication

As we have seen, touch communication can embody a variety of feelings and ideas. The wider the range of meanings for any given type of touch, the greater the potential for misinterpretation. This would suggest that every effort be made to assure that our touches are not misinterpreted. That, of course, is not an easy task. A prime factor influencing interpretation is early childhood training. If our parents have trained us to think of touching as "not nice" or as associated exclusively with sexual activities, then we may have a fundamental conflict in applying other meanings. The area of the body most subject to causing misinterpretation is the hands. Conceivably, a male or female could hold our hand in an intended gesture of friendship. Yet we may tend to withdraw from the communication, perhaps perceiving it as implying sexual interest.

How do we construct an effective method to limit misinterpretation of touch communication? The simplest approach is always the best, and that applies in this case. We introduce touch communication wherever we can, simultaneously with verbal communication. This helps to confirm for the receiver that the message is clear. If, for example, we say to someone, "I want to hug you to wish you well on your trip," as they are departing, the message is clear and should leave little room for misunderstanding. Hugging might also be used to express love, in which case a verbal expression of love would be in place. It is clearly possible that a hug may mean love under one set of circumstances and well wishing under another. Obviously, a key to the meaning of a hug is found in the circumstances and the relationship of the persons involved. Once the meaning of the hug is clear to a specific person under a specific set of circumstances, the words are no longer needed.

## Touch Communication throughout the Life Span

Beginning in infancy, when we were highly dependent on touch as a means of communication, our interactions have had a touch-application-reception factor and a touch-deprivation factor. As babies, our application-reception factor operated at the highest level. We depended upon touching for communication and were highly receptive to it. Primarily, we depended on our mothers for obtaining nourishment, security, safety, love, and the immediate knowledge of our world. We touched our lips and open mouths to their breasts for nourishment. We grasped their fingers and gained more knowledge about our world. We pulled their hair as we explored their bodies and touched their lips and teeth with inquiring hands. Our mothers touched us to clean, change, and console us. As we moved to early childhood, we began to move away from touching interchanges for fulfilling our emotional needs. We progressively accepted speech communication to express and fulfill our needs, abandoning the touch system that had once worked so well.

Our touch-deprivation factor increased as we moved from the first two years of life into adolescence. It is my firm opinion that we do not need to deprive ourselves of the touch communication system. We should be able to bring those earlier faculties along with us as we mature without lessening our ability to communicate verbally. Passage into adolescence and adulthood usually brings with it the tendency to correlate touch with sexual activities and the subsequent loss of the ability to touch spontaneously. Unfortunately, once lost, the ability to touch with meaning, and to accept and understand others' touches, is extremely difficult to regain.

Although touching abilities falter in the early adult years, interest in touching and being touched, as well as the need for it, increases with advancing years in adulthood. Our interest is perhaps sparked by the introduction of new babies into the family, particularly grandchildren. With the new child, we can feel free again to touch, to show love, to express caring and tenderness; touching is the young ones' uninhibited means of relating to others. How often do we see the aged hand of a loving grandparent enfolding the tiny hand of the grandchild? The scene includes a life beginning and a life in the process of ending, each understanding and appreciating the other—not necessarily through words, but through loving touches.

Another reason for our interest in touch in later years is that we tend to experience some loss in those senses that assisted communication via words; our senses of sight and hearing generally become less keen. Eventually, the sense of touch begins to play as important a role as it did in the very beginning. When and if other means of communication are unavailable, we are still able to sense through the skin and to communicate through touching that we feel, that we experience, that we love, that we understand, that we are fully human.

# chapter seven

# Touching for Improving Interpersonal Relationships

Interpersonal relationships form the bases of what we perceive as our state of being. Yet a common complaint today is the alienation workers feel for management, students express about teachers, youth experience with parents, and spouses sense with each other. It seems that despite our efforts to the contrary, our interactions often result in conflict and misunderstanding. On the other hand, our good intentions abound. We wish to give and receive warmth through physical affection. We desire to aid one another in emotional development and self-actualization. We try to maintain an atmosphere in which one individual cares about another's needs and welfare. In short, we care about one another and wish to convey the warmth we feel.

Warmth is a measurable physical quality; however, the type of warmth we are talking about has an internal dimension. How do we derive the concept of "warmth"? In our earliest years, particularly in that period before we developed verbal skills, we depended on tactual senses for a large portion of our learning, coping, and experiencing. We were touched by our parents for consolation, companionship, and protection. Their warm bodies provided us with a feeling of security allowing us to move about with less fear and more emotional strength. Our behavior and adjustment in later life were fundamentally influenced by the degree of emotional warmth we received through our parents' touching. In feeding, bathing, clothing, comforting, and entertaining us, our parents gave us our first concept of love and affection—warmth.

Each of us has the potential for giving physical affection and communicating warmth as we truly seek to improve our interpersonal relations. Our associates, colleagues, and friends also have the need to be touched. They subconsciously have the desire to make human contact, but they may be held back because many of them feel that "it's not nice to touch," or that touching will imply or lead to "something sexual." As individuals in search of a better way to relate to others, we must take the initiative, be slightly daring, and transcend the taboos and unreasonable social restrictions placed on us. We must turn to one of our most natural instincts, the tendency to touch in a caringly human way.

## Touching in Times of Crisis

Have you ever noticed how interpersonal relationships take on more importance in times of crisis? Little children might feel independent as they play outside with their buddies, but an injury will quickly bring them to their parents in search of reassurance and care. Even the momentary crisis experienced by young lovers descending the steepest drop on a roller coaster is enough to trigger the need (or at least the pretext of it) to hold each other securely until the danger passes. Other minor crises include fender-bender auto accidents, final exams, and major business transactions. In any one of these crises, significant persons frequently give us verbal consolation as well as tactual reassurances.

Accordingly, interpersonal relationships are intensified in times of severe crisis, as in interactions between survivors after a death or even between distraught individuals who are separated by long-term physical barriers or divorce. Our friends seek us out more readily when they know we have experienced a crisis. They want us to know that they are close by to help, and they often signal this through touch. Through loving and supportive touches, a person can help to heal a friend's deepest wounds. Touching in such circumstances is something most of us do naturally. Why should we reserve our capability to use touch effectively only for times of crisis? Why not try, in small ways, to build such caring gestures into our day-to-day relationships?

## Touch in Everyday Relationships

If we consider everyday activities in interpersonal relationships, we may see that we have friends and associates with whom we feel more comfortable in communication and touching exchanges. We may not even be aware of the exchanges we engage in; moreover, we may be unconscious of the messages we send out through touch. A case of unconscious touching occurred in the lounge outside a board of trustees' meeting room in a community college in Southern California. Two large lounge chairs were situated side by side, with high armrests close together. A close personal colleague and I sat in the adjoining chairs, placing our hands, parallel and palms down, on the front of each armrest. An active observer, I counted twenty-two contacts from my colleague as we conversed. He would emphasize a point in conversation or assure himself that he had my full attention by reaching over and patting the back of my hand, my forearm, or wrist. During a brief recess in our conversation, I asked him if he had been aware of any touching exchanges while we had been talking. He was surprised to learn that he, a forceful and very masculine character, had been touching the hand of another male. When I explained that I had accepted his touching as a catalyst to communication, he became aware that he could touch another male's hand to improve communication and interpersonal relationships. He later admitted that he had heretofore locked himself (as most Americans do) into the stereotyped role in which touching is generally taboo—especially between males—because of the "sexual overtones" or "sexual connotations." I have a high regard for my colleague because of his ability to accept his natural tendency to touch as a wholesome and useful behavior pattern.

Many of us have similar unconscious habits. If we become more aware of our touching practice, we can learn to use our natural inclinations in a deliberate way to improve interpersonal relationships.

## Touch Can Build Trust

Touching can facilitate a sense of trust and empathy. From early childhood, we begin learning how much we can trust people by the way they touch us. We affix a supreme trust to our parents as we feel their tender and caring touch in feeding, bathing, clothing, and rocking us. Our trust in them stabilizes in proportion to how often they touch us and how often their contact satisfies our needs. Basically, the same commitment to touch is carried forward throughout life; we tend to trust those people whose touching either satisfies our needs or brings us pleasure. The greater the satisfaction received, the greater interest we have in maintaining the touching.

The same dynamics of trust come into play in adult touching experiences. This is particularly true in the helping professions. If we examine very closely why we go to a certain doctor, dentist, or chiropractor, we may find that we are highly influenced by the way these people have touched us and by how much trust they inspired.

Consider your dentist. When you are in the office, seated in the dental chair, you must at least be able to trust that the hands about to treat you will be clean and gentle.

I believe that dentists are acutely aware of the need to communicate trust through touch. They know that patients don't return to dentists who squeeze the inside of their lips to their teeth. Nor do they return to dentists whose novocaine needle hurts more than they imagine the treatment would.

I experienced two contrasting examples of dentists' touching activities. One dentist entered the examination room, shook hands with me warmly, and proceeded to wash his hands in front of me before touching my mouth. Both tactually and visually, his behavior inspired trust. Another dentist neglected both these steps and cleaned my teeth so brusquely that he cut my gum tissues unnecessarily; they bled considerably. Touch and the trust it fosters accounted for the distinctly different impressions these dentists made.

Making a similar point, a woman told me of her experience at a beauty salon over a period of three years. The owner combed and set her hair each week with great care. While the owner washed the woman's hair, she took special interest to see that the strands did not become entangled; she made sure that the roots were not being pulled, nor the ends split, as she combed her hair, and she used a light touch in setting her hair. Mainly in response to the owner's touch, the patron had complete trust in her abilities. Then the owner sold the salon and moved away. The new owner, less cautious, showed little regard for the patron's comfort as she handled her hair. She failed to communicate trustworthiness to her customer and soon lost her.

The effective use of touch to improve relationships requires sensitivity and discretion. As we have seen, though touch has the potential to convey warmth and build trust, it can just as easily produce a tremendous "turn-off."

## Trust in Opposite-Sex Friendships

Clearly, the trustworthiness we communicate can alter our relationships. Our trust in ourselves with regard to touch can also alter relationships. When establishing a new friendship, can you trust yourself to be just friendly and not to expect sexual intimacy with a member of the opposite sex? That's a difficult task for a lot of us. We are so bound by cultural mores that many of us are locked into believing that persons of the opposite sex are not capable of being just good friends; we assume they must eventually become intimate if they maintain a close relationship. In actuality, many people form relationships with members of the opposite sex that do not lead to sexual relations.

A woman account executive of my acquaintance in San Francisco had an experience of this type. She and her friend did not follow the "expected" pattern between men and women. She had attended a business cocktail party where she met a charming man with a lot to say; he startled her with his witty comments, unusual thoughts, and sensitivity. The two later found themselves in her apartment. It was six-thirty in the morning, the sun rising, before they both realized that they had spent the whole night talking, occasionally touching and hugging, experiencing a profound interchange of conversation. They also realized and reflected on the fact that they had not performed the standard antics of a brief conversation followed by a jump into bed, not an uncommon routine for either of them. They agreed to maintain a relationship characterized by the meaningful combination of talking and touching they had enjoyed on their first meeting. Such a relationship requires a high degree of mutual trust and respect. Seven years later, these two people are still enjoying what they consider a most rewarding friendship.

## Building Sexual Relationships

In sexual relationships, persons who exhibit a sexually callous feeling toward others are not apt to be exemplary touchers. Their touches, even though they don't recognize them as such, are mechanical, self-centered, and without concern for the feelings of those they touch. Touchings from the sexually callous are demeaning. The interchange dehumanizes them as well as their partners, because they act as if they were touching inanimate objects—not persons in need of a tactual bridge to dispel their aloneness and reconfirm their humanness. Their touch does not convey a message of loving companionship.

A hierarchy of trust levels applies in all relationships involving touching exchanges, but particularly in romantic relationships. At the beginning level of romantic touching, partners hold hands; the more we hold hands, enjoy the touching, and feel comfortable about it, the more trust we gain in our partner and the more we want to continue holding hands. As trust grows, additional risk is taken, leading to touching and kissing the face, caressing and fondling the breasts, and eventually exploring and caressing the genital area.

If the romantic touching progression moves too quickly, or if it brings pain or fear, the chain of trust can be broken. Frequently, this causes an interruption or discontinuation of touching activities between the two partners. An example of this type of interruption took place in the life of a divorced woman in her early thirties. Alice was married for almost ten years to an energetic Phoenix lawyer; she had been the sexual aggressor, touching and caressing him actively. She felt her marriage broke up because of her aggressiveness in touching exclusively for the purpose of intercourse. After her divorce, she started dating a younger man in his late twenties who had not been married. They became avid hand-holders and were romantically attracted to each other. The two went through the romantic touching progression very slowly and smoothly. That is, the progression was smooth until Alice mistakenly scratched her young mate's genitals, causing a minor abrasion that later became infected. It took several months for her to reestablish a level of trust at which romantic touching could continue.

In the romantic touching progression, we reach a point beyond which we can not move without a profound sense of trust and commitment. If we are going to engage in intimate touching involving sexual relations, we must take responsibility—by mutual agreement—to avoid unwanted pregnancies, pain, add social diseases. Otherwise, we are apt to jeopardize the continued growth of a loving relationship.

A distressing situation occurred wherein one member of a relationship was not able to live up to the original commitment and did not take responsibility for his actions. Hal and Betty were in their middle twenties and were "madly in love." They had established a trusting communication in their sexual relations and seriously planned to be married within a year. Hal worked for an aerospace company in Los Angeles, and during the courtship period, he was called to work for a three-month period at one of the company's branch offices in Texas. After two months, he "became lonely" and found casual sexual companionship with a woman who worked in the Texas plant.

After returning to Los Angeles, he reentered the relationship with Betty, who was unaware of his experience in Texas. After several weeks, Betty began to feel some "unusual pains" in her lower abdomen, accompanied by "an unusual discharge." Her doctor diagnosed a relatively rare social disease that required many months of treatment before a final cure. The disease was traced back to Hal, who thought he had "cured himself," before returning to Los Angeles. The trust in their lovemaking had been reduced so severely that the two lovers, once so fully committed to each other, could not regain their former feelings.

## Don't Think in Stereotypes

An important component to improving interpersonal relationships is developing and maintaining the ability to see people as they *are*—eliminating stereotypes. Sometimes we become rigid in our thinking without realizing it. We tend to suppress our willingness to consider new approaches to thought and behavior patterns, assuming that we don't need new facts or new ideas; our formulated ideas and behavior patterns are the "right ones." This barrier prevents us from growing. It allows us to stereotype other people and makes our critical thinking less effective, our identification of other persons less accurate. Consequently, our interpersonal relationships with the people we have categorized become less effective. For example, if we stereotype a particular person by saying, "He doesn't like to be touched" or "She can't stand to be touched," we tend to behave accordingly; we do not attempt to initiate touching exchanges that could improve the relationship.

Think of the statements: "She likes to be touched" or "He's a toucher." Clearly, such stereotyping statements are subject to many interpretations. If we decide the person referred to is promiscuous, we will treat the individual as such. Conversely, if we interpret the stereotype to mean that the person spoken of enjoys touching for communicating friendship, expressing warm greetings, or conveying empathy, we will direct our behavior toward them in a similar manner. We will seek out their touches when we need expressions of friendship, warm greetings, and empathy. Thus, the judgments we make of others' intentions can influence our behavior in either a negative or positive way. We can prejudge others, locking them into stereotypes that support our desire to move away from them, or we can take a positive attitude and try to move closer.

In either case, our images of others may or may not prove

accurate in real-life situations. We may find those that we categorized as promiscuous touchers don't, in reality, live up to our description of them. Also, those persons that we considered touchers for conveying friendship, greetings, and empathy may prove to have other purposes in mind. Making assumptions about the rationale for someone's touching activities is risky: we cannot be sure of the accuracy of our assessment. Our best approach is to proceed gradually, over a period of time; eventually, though slowly, we will verify or cancel our original judgment.

## Touch in Other Cultures

Tactual expressions are a component of interpersonal relations in all cultures. Every group exhibits some form of touching to express feelings of friendship and love. North and South Americans kiss on the lips, touch cheek to cheek, kiss each other on the cheek, and round it off with hugs. Eskimos, on the other hand, hug rarely and touch noses to express their love. They lightly tap nose to nose, or one partner moves his or her nose in a circular motion around that of the mate, touching it lightly.

Samoans express their most profound love, not by prolonged kissing or touching noses, but by one partner pressing his or her flattened cheek to the cheek of the other party and taking impassioned staccato breaths that cause airjet sounds to emanate from the nose. The staccato pattern also characterizes their sexual relations. Somoans copulate in an abrupt, rapid manner, involving direct contact only between the genitals and almost never including a hug.

Handshake grips also vary according to culture. Segments of the American Black culture shake hands in the following manner: Participant A firmly holds up the palm of one hand, extended at waist level, while participant B slaps A's palm. The palms of both hands come into contact only once, with a loud slapping noise. Afterward, the positions are reversed, with participant A lightly slapping the palms of B. The exchange is also common between athletes and other sports activists.

Some African tribes use an arm grasp in greetings. Participant A extends both forearms, with the hands in a palm-up position and the elbows slightly bent. Meanwhile, participant B places an arm over each of the forearms of A. B's hands then grasp A's forearms at the inside elbow joint. This African arm clasp might well be considered as an alternative to the standard Western handshake to avoid some of its disadvantages. The standard handshake appears to have little meaning other than a cursory recognition of the individual. We might bring about a benevolent revolution by examining the various ways of revealing warmth, determining the effects of passivity in the exchange, measuring the relationship between the pressure applied and the meanings given (or received), and determining the significance of varying types of grasps and embraces. Such a study could give us some new insights and a refreshing perspective on how to use touch to express friendship and love.

## Touching and Self-Disclosure

Touching holds much promise as a mode of communicating feelings and emotions. In fact, research shows that there is a correlation between touching and self-disclosure (Lomranz and Shapira 1974). The more we enter interpersonal relationships that include touching behavior, the more willing we become to disclose ourselves. Conversely, the more capable we are of self-disclosure, the more open we are to touching exchanges. Both activities are characteristic of effective interpersonal communications and are reliable indicators of movement toward closer relationships.

## Improving Relationships Through Touching Behavior

Attempts to improve interpersonal relationships through touch in female pairs have a higher potential for improvement than those in male pairs (Walker 1975). Our society seems to accept the fact that female friends kiss each other on the cheek, hold hands, or walk arm in arm together. But how rare it is to see a male kiss another male on the cheek, hold hands, or have any sustained tactual contact. Touching actions to improve relationships between males are primarily limited to the handshake, a pat on the back, some light punches to the arms and shoulders, or games that allow socially permissible touching. Women can more efficiently and effectively use touching to improve relationships. Yet they generally associate touching with sexual activity and feel more comfortable if their touching is directed to the opposite sex. The males in our country also associate touching with feminine acts, like women touching other women or women touching men. Men thus hesitate to touch other men, feeling their identity might be questioned if they behaved in a manner perceived as feminine.

Clearly, in female pairs as well as in male pairs, there are socially acceptable foundations from which to begin when seeking to deepen a relationship through touch. Female friends may wish to discuss how they feel about their current touching behavior. Are they involved with each other in touching ways that enhance their friendship? Can they become more involved in touch for improving greetings and recognition of one another without causing discomfort or allowing unwanted sexual overtones to intrude? Is there a way in which male pairs can demonstrate comradeship, friendliness, and admiration through more profound handshakes? Perhaps they can agree on an arm grip that doesn't convert their heterosexuality into an appearance of homosexuality.

Touching occurs more frequently between opposite-sex

friends than between same-sex friends. Opposite-sex friends' touching, however, occurs under more limited conditions and in more restricted locations (Walker 1975). In such relationships, although women are more prone to self-disclosure, men are more often the initiators of touching exchanges (Lomranz and Shapira 1974). The aggressive position of males in touching has not helped them to become very adept at self-disclosure however. Women tend to disclose themselves more, to other women as well as to men. They also tend to increase the amount of disclosure as a result of trusting touch exchanges more than men do. Because of women's relative openness, men have a greater potential for improving their relationships with women through touch than they do with other men.

## Difficulties in Touching Strangers

Touching to improve interpersonal relations cannot occur so easily between strangers. Most of us are not very open to touch as part of our communicating. A limitation that is even more pronounced among strangers. Basically, we are not a touching society, and we tend to feel discomfort in most touching interactions. Factors that contribute to this are (1) our basic lack of trust in strangers and (2) our resistance to being observed in touching interactions. We frequently have unverified suspicions about strangers, so we tend to proceed very cautiously with them, especially when it comes to touching. Although the handshake is generally an acceptable opening gesture in meeting a stranger, some people are reluctant to extend a hand to someone they do not know. This reluctance can be seen in churches where a handshake is part of the ritual; resistance is sometimes expressed as an actual refusal. Whatever the reasons for this resistance, it is clear that interpersonal relating must be entered into willingly; moreover, the imposition of a touching exchange can have an adverse effect. In some areas, congregational resistance to shaking hands has brought about a compromise from the pulpit. Religious leaders are asking their congregations to recognize their fellow church members by alternate modes: smiling or simply verbalizing a greeting.

We resist being observed in touching actions, perhaps mostly because we envision a sexual link to touching. Our cultural mores prohibit us from observing the most intimate form of touching—sexual intercourse. We extend our reluctance to being observed to many signs of affection, whether or not they are sexual in intent. As mature adults, we shy away from hugging or embracing in public, even for expressing friendship.

Modern psychologists have sought out ways through encounter group sessions to modify our behavior to allow us to feel more open to nonverbal touching behavior. Conflicting views have been presented. Allen (1967) and Koch (1971) tell us that most touching techniques used in encounter groups are of little benefit, perhaps even harmful, since they foster defensiveness, produce stress, and have a potential for being psychologically disturbing. Their position underscores our cultural trait of little openness to touching strangers. It also points to a reluctance to have touching activities observed. I strongly recommend, however, that we consider a progressive, slowly developing, step-by-step pattern of touching behavior for specific purposes that would allow us to transcend the discomfort associated with touching strangers in general, while enabling us to relax just a bit about our touching behavior.

Understandably, most of us are not ready to embrace a complete stranger on the first meeting. If we are interested in developing a relationship, we want more information to go on. The information can generally be gained through verbal exchanges, which are more distant, less threatening, and more easily controlled than tactual contact. We can generally determine, through conversation, if we wish to move closer to others, and we can slowly assess their trustworthiness as they simultaneously determine ours.

If we are consistent in the meanings of our touching behavior, and others are similarly consistent with us, an unthreatening progression will follow. We will know, as will they, that a light touch by a hand on the arm is an act of friendliness and an expression of interest, not one of hostility or aggression. We can progressively work out understandings, such as whether a pat on the knee is used to show playfulness, to emphasize a point, or even to express a greeting. We can communicate that a hug or a full embrace means a warm greeting (a commitment of the entire self to it, so to speak), not sexual aggression. All touching transactions, in order not to threaten the relationship, must proceed with moderation and clearly expressed intentions.

## Begin with Those Closest to You

A healthy improvement in the ability to be comfortable about touching might be brought about through slow, progressive, deliberate acts. This certainly doesn't mean that we become touching exhibitionists, ready to show everybody that we are the world's greatest touchers. A good place to begin could be in our homes. How many friends have confided that they never saw their parents hold hands, hug, or kiss each other? This state of affairs obviously encourages the children's future reticence to express themselves through touch. I suggest that couples begin to express their caring through touch in their homes freely, regardless of who is watching. Children or others who observe might be surprised or possibly ill at ease about what they see, viewing it as a departure from "dignified" behavior; but after several observations, they will probably be able to regard it as the honest expression of affection and caring it is. Don't hesitate on this; it is worth the risk. It can gradually make your life richer with meaning and expressed feelings.

Let's start with those people who are very significant in our lives. If they are a part of the family, very close friends, or loving mates, they will be more accepting of this new idea. Next time you are in conversation with one of them, place a hand on your loved one's upper forearm. Just leave your hand there for a few seconds, and then draw it away. Note the reaction. Try to do this without being too obvious. If the recipient draws away or resists the idea of being touched, explain your new concept of showing interest through touch.

Without giving notice, take your mate's hand. Say nothing. Just hold the hand as unobtrusively as possible for a few minutes; then go back to doing whatever you were doing before. Or take your child lightly in your arms at intervals during the day. Let the child return to play or study without entering into verbal exchanges. The next time you are with a colleague you admire, dare to go over and give the associate a light pat on the back, saying, "You know, I really enjoy working with you" or "It's really great to be here with you." All these recommendations are designed to aid in improving interpersonal relationships. If our honest intent is to improve, we will do so. To gauge our progress, we might make "before" and "after" assessments of our relationships during a six-month period; a greater trust will surely emerge.

Touching behavior can have a significant impact on interpersonal relationships. Our touches and tactual expressions, when applied appropriately and tactfully, can carry with them a sense of warmth and companionship. Touches tend to improve interactions and communications. They cement our social and personal bonding with those people who are special to us.

# chapter eight

# Touching for Loving and Making Love

Loving relationships falter and frequently fail because those involved cannot identify what love is, what it includes. We have all heard that love is an abstract thought or emotion without a definition. We are told that love is just something we "feel" or that it just "happens" to us as if we had no control over it. The truth is that love is definable; it is a fundamental choice that is expressed in everyday acts, thoughts, and feelings. Loving gestures are an essential aspect of love because they communicate it in a concrete way.

## Loving Relationships Include Touching

Loving relationships, in order to be specific and concrete, must include specific and mutually acceptable actions and extensive sharing of feelings and thoughts. For some of us, mutually acceptable actions in loving relationships include tactual expressions that are not necessarily directed exclusively to sexually specific goals. Loving relations may well include heartfelt handshakes, happy and cordial hugs, and jovial and friendly pats on the back and forearms. These types of gestures, plus friendly kisses on the cheek and affectionate pecks on the lips, all play an important role in loving relations as long as both parties involved are clear as to their meaning.

By no means must loving relationships be based on just a physical feeling resulting from tactual exchanges. They are founded on shared attitudes, beliefs, and self-reflections (Zastrow and Chang 1977). The relationship is not just irrational and centered on feeling. It is rational because it is based on thought that causes the actions, touching or otherwise, and the feelings. This view of loving relationships is perhaps startling for many of us, as it suggests that the relationship is not "just something that happened" but something that we can make happen. Consider the following example: Two persons, A and B, encounter each other and begin to get acquainted. Person A reflects: "She thinks as I do. She interests me." This is followed with the thought: "I have a good feeling about this person. I like her very much." Person A created these thoughts in his own mind; they are not just ideas, thoughts, and feelings that simply happened or came exclusively from some outside, unknown, and uncontrollable source. In the same way, he can create other thoughts and emotions just as easily to replace them. Thus, we have the potential for creating, modifying, or adding to our loving relationships. We can "determine" our relationships.

An important ingredient in loving relations is the ability to play (Kalish 1967). This is not surprising when we consider that healthy childhood development is dependent on play to provide opportunities to enter our first social relationships with peers. Our first experiences with play are those we encounter alone. This first solo play involves extensive tactual activity with objects like blocks, teddy bears, dolls, balls, balloons, swings, and almost any object that attracts us and is easily manipulated. After we become accustomed to playing with our own things, we enjoy having another child around. This parallel play does not include tactual interacting except when scuffles break out over toys. At some time between two and three years of age, we begin to play with other children of the same age. This interaction allows us to use our imaginations, imitate our parents, and establish our first loving relations with peers in a childlike fashion. At this time, we may even attempt to imitate our parents by initiating tactual experiments that suggest some future behavior.

Aggressive feelings may be released through playing, there may not be opportunities for them to be expressed in any other way. A little girl playing with her doll may wish to imitate her mother and give the doll the same whacks she receives from her mother. The imitation play allows the child to take on her mother's role and have her mother's authority. Playing roles can be reversed when the child wishes to "be the baby" so he or she can receive caressing strokes and tender cuddling from an imaginary mother.

Playing in loving relationships can lead the participants to new learning. It offers people the opportunity to learn new and different methods of getting along with each other and to improve motor skills and verbal and nonverbal communication. Play also provides excitement and exercise, as well as healthy parent-child, child-child, and adult-adult relationships.

If we are to develop a rational, loving relationship at any age, we must consider how clear we are about our own needs, desires, and goals (Zastrow and Chang 1977). We must become knowledgeable about the individual who may become our partner. We must assure ourselves that our thoughts and feelings about that potential partner are realistic and rational. We should have full knowledge of the other person and feel free to communicate with him or her openly and honestly. Loving relationships are highly dependent upon each partner's ability to think clearly and communicate openly; as communication succeeds, so will the relationship.

Simple touching actions can convey caring and loving

messages that are not sexually specific. On meeting someone for the first time, we can send a message like, "You are a nice person; I like you," through a pat on the arm or a tap on the shoulder. While shaking the person's hand, we can pat the back of the hand lightly implying, "Great pleasure to know you" or "I hope we get to know each other better." The first handshake is much more significant in initiating loving relationships than we may realize. There are subtle messages that we send by the warmth of the handshake, the texture of our hands. Even the pressure we apply may begin a loving relationship; it may also cause the first meeting to be the last one. Have you ever shaken hands with someone who had cold, clammy palms? Contact with hands like that does not encourage further interest, just as bone-crushing grips do not make good impressions. Our handshake represents our personality, at least in the mind of the person on the receiving end. Our hands convey the message that we are "cold and clammy" or "warm, friendly, and loving" people.

Unfortunately, we are not sure of how our handshake comes across to others. Very few of us meet others who tell us about our "clammy hands" or "crushing clasp." It would be a good idea to suggest among friends that everyone shake hands; then have individuals take turns rating the warmth of others' handshakes. In the process, tips for improving one's own handshake might emerge.

By careful attention and thoughtful actions, we should never allow any of our touching approaches to become stressful situations for new friends. There must be mutual acceptability in tactual expressions, or they may lead to stressful communications that are considered invasions of another's privacy. Initiating almost any touching relationship on a first meeting is difficult because of potential sexual implications. Loving relationships are not always converted into or intended to be the same as sexual relationships, and this distinction, sometimes very fine, can create a difficulty.

Timing is important. Its significance can easily be tested.

Shake someone's hand, but instead of releasing it as usual, hold onto the hand for one minute. Observe the reaction. The longer your grasp exceeds the expected few seconds, the more discomfort and uncertainty you can expect the other person to experience. Handshaking has its time limit. Our cultural behavior patterns prescribe the two-to-three-second handshake for most social situations. Each of us has adopted this time pattern in handshakes. Handshakes of five to eight seconds are usually found in loving situations. They take a little more time and are more attention getting, and they are not viewed as perfunctory acts like routine handshakes. Handshakes that last beyond eight to ten seconds are usually identified as "holding hands" and are considered more intimate. More often, they are used in communicating a sexual approach. For many of us, they are foreplay to the sex act.

Like the handshake, touches to the forearms and shoulders that last more than two to three seconds are not perceived as perfunctory acts. If these gestures continue for more than eight seconds, they are generally perceived as a loving act. When we maintain continual contact beyond eight to ten seconds, the gesture may be perceived as approaching an intimate relationship leading to sexual foreplay.

### Parental Relationship as a Model for Loving

Loving touches are those touches we learned about as infants and children. They were not touches leading to sexual intercourse but maternal and paternal touches that were, and still can be, expressive of tenderness and care. Actually, loving relationships most naturally exist when two individuals need each other. Lovers, or would-be lovers—anxious in their needs and those of their mates but confused about their roles or about love itself—would benefit by looking to their initiation into human relations. Loving relationships are founded on an awareness of the needs and vulnerability of the loving partners, as conveyed through signs of sincere concern, tenderness, and active responsibility for each other. As infants, if we are cuddled, caressed, and tenderly handled, we receive the tactual communication that we are loved. It is from these early experiences that we learn to cuddle and caress, to express our love of other persons. This does not suggest that touching, loving relationships, to become effective, require one partner to play the role of the child and the other, the role of the parent. Let us adapt the parent-child model of touching to an adult-adult relationship. In other words, let's use those beautiful tactual experiences we learned from our parents. We have the biological need for them throughout our lives. However, we tend to cut them off or severely limit them by the time we reach the age of twelve or thirteen.

Starting with our first experience with parent-infant cuddling, we have the potential to convert our early touchings to an adult-adult form of embrace. After many years of parent-child cuddling, we learned of the security and comfort such contact could bring. We always knew that we could turn to the arms of a parent, or parent substitute, and have our distress and fears hugged away. There were no sexual implications associated with those huggings and holdings. They were sheer loving relationships. There were no conditions tied to them. They were open; they were free; they were available in abundance. Those of us who received them in abundance remember them well and reflect gratefully on the serenity and security they brought us. That feeling can still be ours through loving touching relationships.

Location is important for determining and acting out loving relationships through touching. Social setting and placement of body contact are components of location. Many societies have been able to adapt parent-child cuddling touches to adult-adult loving relationships without difficulty. To be successful, though, training must begin early in the life of the child. The model the child sees in adult-adult hugging relationships must be sincere and convey that the contact has meaning. An embrace of this type is a part of social custom in most Latin American countries. Family members and good friends exchange embraces. Occasions for embraces are generally arrivals and departures from one another. Men embrace men and women alike, and women do the same. The embrace consists of pressing the shoulders of one partner to the shoulders of the other. Each gently pats the other on the back for two to three seconds. As a rule, the total embrace lasts no more than five to eight seconds, and there is no cheek-to-cheek contact. The exchange carries no sexual overtones, and neither participant allows the lower part of the body or the genital area to come into contact. This expression is very reflective of earlier, parent-child hugging relationships. The modifications for an adult-adult hugging relationship include duration and the extent of body contact.

Parent-infant kissing is suggestive of a loving relationship. When a parent kisses the infant or child on the cheeks, lips, or body, he or she is expressing feelings of love without suggesting a sexual relationship. The duration and placement of the kisses indicate the meaning and purpose of the contact. Parent-child kissing generally is directed to the head, forehead, cheeks, and, with some parents, to the lips. Unfortunately, this meaningful contact is discouraged and, in most cases, either radically reduced or abolished after the child reaches the age of twelve or thirteen. At that age, our cultural pressures push us into a new perspective. We are led to believe that all kissing is an entrée, an act offering privileged approaches to sexual intercourse. Accepting these cultural pressures and adapting our behavior patterns to meet them stymies our relationships. We can convert parent-infant kissing into adult-adult kissing. As adults, we still need loving relationships as much as we did in childhood. Kissing one another in appropriate, affectionate, nonsexual ways is a tactual act we should be able to carry through our teens and relish in adulthood. Such acts are meaningful. They allow us to express completely our loving nature and receive the similar expressions we so deeply need.

Parent–infant hand-holding is another loving gesture. The touch and guidance of this childhood experience helped us learn to cross streets safely, or venture into the ocean or a swimming pool for the first time. Hand-holding with our parents carried with it no overtones of sexual intimacy. It was simply a loving gesture. Little boys held their father's hands, and little girls held their mothers' hands without any hints of homosexuality. At the crucial age of twelve or thirteen, we learned through observation that boys don't hold boys' hands, just as girls don't hold girls' hands. To the teenager seeking independence, hand-holding begins to suggest dependency. The role of independence, at least the cultural expression of that role, becomes more highly valued than the parent–child expression of a loving relationship. Giving in to this cultural pressure, and subsequently giving up the hand-to-hand contact, leaves a tremendous gap in our lives. As adults, we continue to walk down many unknown paths, many roads of insecurity, and if we are able to take those passages with someone we trust and love as we loved our parents, we can regain that feeling of security that is so important to well-being.

Texture and temperature are important in conveying love. Soft, pliable hands and lips remind us of our mothers. In later life, we associate such touches with similar touches we received as children, touches that conveyed supreme support and affection. Childhood lyrics aptly express the opposite type of experience: "Cold hands, warm heart, dirty feet, and no sweetheart." In other words, the texture of dirty feet and the temperature of cold hands do not facilitate loving. In infancy and childhood, parental hands and lips that touched and caressed us were pleasantly warm; at the very least, they were about the same temperature as our own body and not discomfortingly cold. Our preference for warmth is carried over into adulthood. A warm handshake, even a brief holding of a warm hand, and a warm kiss to cheeks or lips are tactually associated with earlier loving relationships. We will benefit greatly in improving our relationships if we can offer the lover the texture and temperature that most of us enjoyed as children.

## Love in a Sexual Relationship

For the past decade, the media—through magazines, books, movies, and even lectures—have given us more than most of us wanted to know about "lovemaking" or "making love." The subject has been researched, analyzed, talked about, put in the spotlight on national television, and featured at the local X-rated movie theater. Lovemaking has become widely discussed, dissected in the classroom, demonstrated in "live shows" from San Francisco to the East Coast, and exhibited on the main street in Honolulu.

For the most part, the worldwide exhibition of the "art of love" has not brought added meaning to the sex lives of curious investigators. Most people who have sought out a greater knowledge on "how to make love" have gained "tactical" information. That is, we have learned all the positions for lovemaking and all the different approaches to the opposite sex, but we have not learned what we feel about these "positions" and "approaches." For most of us, the exploitation of making love by the media reveals only the mechanical side of sex. X-rated movies have featured close-ups of coital positions and exchanges of oral sex, but little has been revealed about the "feeling" side other than: "It feels good" or "It must feel good; they are doing it, aren't they?" The "why" and the "how you feel about it" of lovemaking have been left out of most demonstrations and descriptions. In discussing touches for making love, the remaining portion of this chapter reviews touching actions as they relate to feelings and meaning in a relationship. To be most enjoyable and rewarding, touches must be given and received with the intention of expressing love and a serious commitment toward one's partner. For this reason, it will be most helpful to review some concepts of love before we seek to create a perspective on such touches.

Everyone has a definition of love. Just ask around, and you will find almost as many definitions as you find people who wish to define it. There is "friendly love," "family-love," "platonic love," "puppy love," and "passionate love." Some say that love is an emotion that has no limits. For the romantic, this may be acceptable, but for "rational love," there appear to be specific boundaries. Sufficient time for expressing love is a condition that allows it to flourish. If we do not have the time, and are not willing or capable of making the time, love will not flourish. Time is needed for love to grow. A second ingredient of rational love is nearness. There must be a desire to experience and enjoy the nearness of the loved one. Long periods of estrangement, being away emotionally and/or physically, are a detriment. We must be close and have a strong need and desire to maintain closeness, for if we are not with the loved one, we shall not know love.

Love is in constant motion. It increases and decreases as circumstances and environment affect it. We change our concept of love and of loved ones as they interact with us. The more we offer love to a mate, the more it replenishes itself. Loving relations endure only as long as the recipients act in a reciprocal manner. Loving feelings must be mutual, if not, the relationship deteriorates.

Love is offered in freedom. Love cannot exist by force or mandate. No law or contract can ensure that one will either love or continue to love another person. Love is a choice; one *decides* to love. Love offers forgiveness and tolerance; it encourages compromises. Love includes acceptance of the other. It excludes even a temporary interest in vengeance against a loved one. Love is not withheld if one person ceases to behave properly or to please the other. The withdrawal of love is not threatened as a means of controlling the other.

Lovers are the facilitators of happiness, not the sole sources. Both lovers consider the needs and desires of their mates, but neither is ultimately responsible for the other's happiness. Love is dependent on emotional growth, and our ability to love and be loved is never static; it passes through many stages. In maturity, we have a greater chance to realize the depth of love.

Sexual attraction is often mistaken for love. It may bring potential lovers together, but it does not assure that love will grow, that real caring will result from the sexual experience. Love flourishes in an atmosphere of patient endearment and unselfish acts with the freely chosen person who is the recipient of our affection. Love is not something that just happens; it is a decision of commitment that is demonstrated through faithful interaction with another person. Sexual attraction may bring two people together, but love, to nourish itself, must include an ongoing exchange of creativity.

## First Youthful Attempts at Making Love

The preteen years are filled with fantasies and interest in touches for love. These years are those in which we begin a new search for tactual sensitivity. In infancy, our loving touches were converted and transformed into voice communication. We accepted our mother's tone of voice and caring words as substitutes for her earlier loving touches. Particular words and a special tone of voice conveyed certain meaning and emotions. Our mother's words, harsh or loving, began to have the same effect on us as her touches had before; we applied meaning and feeling to the words. From our fifth to eleventh years, we relied more on verbal communication. The magic age of puberty, however, brings with it an even greater need to be touched and to touch. The need stems from our renewed search for acceptance, comfort, and intimacy. A revitalized search for the meaning of tactuality within our bodies sparks the interest. Our genitals become more sensitive to touch, and we begin to explore that sensitivity to learn its ranges and dimensions, to understand it. We have heard about sexual kisses and sexual touches from "more experienced" peers who glow with the news of their intimacies. Our attraction to the idea of touching another's genitals is spurred by curiosity and the daring feeling of doing something forbidden. We experience a driving force to know the unknown. Some of us participate in sexual touching, even engage in comprehensive sexual acts, before our teens. This is not to suggest that we engage in sexual acts that represent loving touches at this time.

Most of the first touches of young people are relatively mechanical and whimsical. At this time, the goal is to answer the question: "Can I do it?" or "I wonder if I'll be allowed to touch him or her there?" The experience is often referred to as "feeling around," and young males tend to be more active participants. Even though sexual touchings are "forbidden," the "red-blooded American" male excuses the forbidden acts as only doing what comes naturally. They set a pattern for progressively more sex touching. Meanwhile, the young female is aware that her participation in sexual acts may win her a "bad reputation" and, even worse, may vastly change her entire life course if they result in pregnancy. The boy who scores is a hero, and the girl is an "easy mark."

The tactics of the sex-touch pattern of young males usually begin with abundant and progressively more aggressive mouth-to-mouth kissing. Kisses are sustained for an increasing period of time, and exploration of the mouth with the tongue follows the kissing. Tongue-to-tongue stimulation heightens the excitement for each partner. Each may take turns placing his or her tongue in the other's mouth. The exploring tongue usually finds its way beneath the partner's tongue; it passes over the teeth and gums.

The young male moves an inquiring hand and fingertips over the face and neck of his partner. If there appears to be no resistance to touches around the neck, the next areas to be explored are the female's breasts. Touching their partner's breasts is the first major hurdle for most males. On the first occasion, it is done with much forethought; the act might be rejected. If the female rejects the touch, the petting pattern may not continue or may cease altogether. An interlude may follow in which there is an opportunity to clarify the purpose and meaning of the touching. It is more likely, however, if the new experiment feels good, that there will be an unspoken agreement to continue the contact. Some young couples rationalize, "If it feels OK and doesn't hurt anyone to do it, then it's okay." Many unmarried women see the situation from another perspective, with thoughts like: "If I permit such touching, I might be encouraging this guy to go all the way, and then people will say I have only myself to blame if he 'loses control'." Other young women seek out breast fondling, recognizing it as a preliminary step to sexual intercourse, and they welcome it for that reason. Some young women feel well prepared (though in reality they may not be) to accept all the intimacies of sexual touching, particularly if they have taken steps for birth control.

The youth of today are not as naive about sexual intimacies as they were a decade or two ago. They tend to be more open to tactual experiences leading to intercourse. In previous generations, petting without intercourse was the means of sexual outlet; it was one of the most enjoyable and perhaps one of the greatest pastimes of American youth. In contemporary society, the word *petting*, as well as the act, has lost much of its earlier prominence. Modern attitudes toward birth control abound, but technology is lagging. More recent data on harmful side effects of the pill have left our youth without a safe, reliable contraceptive. Diaphragms and condoms are generally considered chancy in view of tragic increases in teenage motherhood. Petting has been replaced by foreplay and intercourse. Youth of today verbalize this difference in perspective with questions like, "Why should I limit myself to the simple preliminaries like petting, when I can find a partner who wants to go all the way?"

For those young couples who continue to pet as a means of

**111**

sexual expression, the experience serves an important educational function. With an effective petting partner, we will have a greater chance of becoming more effective as a loving sexual partner in marriage. Premarital petting, with its progressive nature, offers each partner the opportunity to learn to relax in intimate relationships. There is a relaxed feeling that the gradual kissing and touching that move from the head toward the genitals will proceed in an orderly fashion, that there will be no abrupt changes in the style of kissing and touching. The slow, progressive touching creates an atmosphere that helps to relax the muscles. The body, particularly the female body, becomes progressively more ready to accept and participate in full coitus. Females who do not experience these progressive petting touches prior to marriage are more apt to become tense in their sexual relations, particularly in those that are hastily undertaken and do not allow for a progression to a mood of readiness.

A disadvantage of petting is the tremendous buildup of readiness for coitus it creates when the couple has agreed not to proceed to the sexual act. Youth who depend on petting as their only sexual release find that it leaves them with a feeling of tension. They have pleasant sensations but also a frustrated feeling of "having no place to go." After some hesitancy and deliberation, they may find a satisfactory means, short or actual coitus of bringing each other to climax, such as through manual or oral stimulation.

When we are new at lovemaking, we "try out" many types of kisses and intimate touches. In each of these experiences, we are seeking to learn both what it feels like and how to do it. As we all remember, learning about sexual relating by "doing," and at the same time expressing romantic feelings toward the partner, as well as seeking to formulate personal values about lovemaking is like a sublime juggling act, to which we devote much of our energy during adolescence. The energy is well spent, though, because these experiences prepare us for participation in meaningful sexual relations as adults. It is most important that the young person combine the search for meaning and for loving relationships with sexual exploration; this overall activity comprises a major developmental task of adolescence and young adulthood.

## Kisses in Lovemaking

We can use genital sensitivity to hurt, harm, or exploit others. We can use it to affirm or reject our masculinity or femininity. Ideally, we use it to transmit feelings of love that we could not effectively communicate verbally.

An expressive touch of love must be given in warmth and sincerity. This delicate type of touch becomes ineffectual if presented in disguise. Touches of love will not "ring clear" or be received as meaningful expressions if they are given or received in emotional pretense. A simple kiss can be an expressive touch of love. A kiss can also be used to manipulate the feelings of others for some advantage, but the disguise is easily detected by most sensitive persons.

The shape, curvature, texture, and natural moisture of the lips combine to make the act of kissing among the most effective and sensitive means of expressing love. A quick lip-to-lip touch between two partners can communicate a simple "hello" or a wish for a greater loving exchange. The message is in the intent. A kiss is an open expression, and the meaning it is intended to communicate is not always clear to the recipient. Partners involved in ongoing relationships can learn more easily to read the signals in a kiss. They become more adept at using kissing for greetings and recognition, as well as to initiate lovemaking.

A comprehensive means of expressing endearment, kissing may be extended to practically all parts of the loved one's body. As infants and children, most of us received an abundance of kisses applied to the forehead, occasionally to the top of the head, and to cheeks and lips. If these kisses were given by parents and other significant persons and we received them as expressions of endearment and caring, we are more likely to appreciate similar kisses from an adult partner. For such persons, loving kisses can be applied to the rest of the body with similar meaning. Of course, a greater sense of intimacy occurs in adult kissing. Lips are dramatically expressive; they can carry affective tactual messages that are often difficult, if not impossible, to relay in verbal communication. A kiss can tell of the tenderness of the loving relationship, of the strength of the bond between two lovers, and of the intensity of the sentiments and the commitment shared. Thus, to become a caring human act, kissing must be used to share feelings, not just to induce intercourse.

No two lovers are alike in their approach to kissing. One individual may prefer the mate's lips to be dry; the mate's saliva may be considered vulgar and generally unclean. Another lover may prefer wet lips. Most loving individuals prefer lightly moistened lips. The contact with the loving partner's lips is then smoother and allows for an easy and pleasant sliding motion in exchanging caresses. It is most helpful for both partners to explain their preference for one condition or another. The pressure and variety of kisses should be mutually satisfying to both lovers. The relationship will be enhanced by combining passionate intensity with warmth and affection. In new loving relationships, neither lover will know the intensity of the other's kisses, and both will adapt or modify their kissing behavior to please each other.

Varieties and locations of kisses abound. There are as many ways of kissing as there are persons to think them up. And there are just as many places to apply kissing as there are spots on the human body to receive it. A straight, closed-mouth, wet-lip kiss is among the most common modes. An open-mouth, exploring kiss is popular among less conservative lovers. The open mouth is generally associated with a more inclusive relationship and suggests a greater receptivity to tongue-to-tongue touching and to open-mouth kissing of the breast and genitals. Repeated, short, closed-mouth, "peck" kissing can carry an adoring message, whereas long kisses are for intense lovers who enjoy prolonged contact. Each lover enjoys ample time to explore the lips, mouth, and tongue of the other. In many cases, the mouth and tongue serve as simulated sex organs.

Sense receptors in the mouth, lips, breasts, and genitals appear to be most responsive to the contact of kissing lips. These areas are highly sensitive to moist, smooth stimulation, particularly that of lips and the delicate touch of a caressing tongue. Once the lips and mouth are satiated, many lovers proceed to caress the neck and the chest or breasts of their loved one. Each of the lovers may take the active role in applying kisses to the upper abdomen. The senses of the entire body are awakened with these caresses. Any of the kissing modes used in lip-to-lip kissing may be applied to the upper body and evoke pleasant and sexually loving feelings. The female breast becomes the focal point of kissing in this area. Kisses can cover the entire breast and usually are applied to the areola and nipples. Such kisses are often stimulating and pleasurable, and the male frequently progresses to a sucking action. Reminiscent of infancy, this sucking is now reintroduced, not to seek the nurturance of food, but to express nurturing for love. Many males also enjoy light tonguing and sucking of their nipples. Lovers who are willing to discuss their likes and dislikes can improve their relationships by discovering more effective, comforting, and acceptable touching techniques. Both the partners will experience personal growth and increasing closeness to each other from such exchanges.

Kissing the central part of the body is a valuable experience in loving relations. Not only is it a pleasurable experience for both partners, but it brings about a greater awareness of each other's body—its contours, sensitivities, and skin texture. The navel is an alluring opening for most people. Contact there is pleasure giving and erotic. The navel is sensitive to touches from the lips and tongue, and many loving couples find ways to enhance contacts to this area through careful exploration.

Applying kisses to the genitals is a tender and exciting show of full affection for lovers. The first experience of oral-genital contact may be somewhat threatening to new lovers if the act has been associated heretofore with derogatory and demeaning types of behavior. However, kissing the genitals of a loving partner is much more common than was once believed. Committed lovers tend to use this contact to express that commitment and a desire to enhance their mate's pleasure. The male lover will frequently introduce oral-genital kissing by moving his lips from the central part of the body over and around the public hair to the vaginal crevice. A light moist kiss may first be applied to the upper part of the crevice, directly to the hood covering the clitoris. The inner and outer lips of the vagina are highly sensitive to oral stimulation. The female lover may begin oral-genital kissing by lightly touching the sides of the penis with her lips and continuing the kisses in an up-and-down motion to each side of the shaft. Oral stimulation of the crown and head of the penis and of the testicles is stimulating and pleasurable for the male. Each couple determines through experimentation which types of oral-genital caresses, if any, are acceptable and mutually pleasurable. The results of Kinsey's studies suggest that such oral stimulation is enjoyed by most loving couples (Kinsey 1953).

After we explore and learn all the different ways to kiss, led on by curiosity or recommendations from peers or sex manuals, we can perpetuate the kisses without realizing that they can become mechanical. Most unfortunately, we can learn all the motor skills that permit us to kiss in a loving exchange but still fail to kiss with feeling or meaning. We are then stupefied if asked, "What did you mean by that kiss?"

As with all modes of communication, the meaning of a kiss can only be transmitted effectively if it carries the same meaning for the sender and the receiver. For this reason, verbal communication in conjunction with kissing is helpful. The warmest, most intense regard of one person for another, potentially reaching a spiritual quality, may be expressed through a kiss given at the right moment and under the right circumstances. A kiss can be (and is, for those who wish it to be) a symbolic expression of warm feelings, affection, and endearment. It can express the desire to be loved and the desire to give love, representative of joy in mutual sharing. When such meaning is applied to pleasure-filled and sexually arousing kisses to the entire body, the result can be a relationship approaching the sublime.

## Caresses for Lovemaking

An affectionate embrace is one of the most comprehensive ways of expressing love. A full embrace allows a wider range of contact with more of the body, specifically those areas on the cheeks, lips, breasts, and genitals that are more sensitive to erotic stimulation. In a full embrace, we can touch lips with our partner's lips and move the entire body—breast to breast and genitals to genitals—in a delicate, sensual motion that will create a sensation both sexually erotic and sensually loving.

Lightly stroking the body in a rhythmical way is pleasing, just as open-fingered stroking of the hair and scalp can stimulate one's partner. Stroking the shoulders, letting the fingers rotate and seek the curvature of the mate's muscles, is another personal and tender message of love. Many men particularly enjoy this touch because it acknowledges the male physique. Cupping the breast in the hand and stroking it in a light, rotating fashion are delightful for most men and women. While men enjoy the prolonged contact with a woman's breast, the women receive recognition and stimulation from the messagelike touch. Nipples of both men and women are sensitive to touch. Placing the nipples between the thumb and index finger and squeezing lightly is just one of many varieties of touches to the breast. Care should be taken not to squeeze too hard, for the breasts are very sensitive. On first engaging in such touching, one should ask the partner for feedback. The partner should have the chance to indicate which motions and pressures feel best.

Palming the buttocks and rotating them in one's hands is a delightful experience. The texture of the skin and tissues of the buttocks are soft and pliable and provide warm sensations when gently kneaded by a loving partner. The kneading action can be varied in pressure and location to give the most pleasing effect.

Manual touches to the genitals should proceed with thoughtful caution and concern. It is so easy, even when one wants to be gentle, to bring pain instead of pleasure. As in all loving touches, the hands should be clean and well-groomed. Rough-edged fingernails should be cut and filed smooth beforehand. Even small skin calluses can cause painful irritations to the genitals; they should be rubbed away with an emery board to assure that the touch will be a tender caress and not a scratchy stroke. Running the tips of the fingers lightly through the public hair can arouse interest in more extensive genital touching and can build confidence in the pleasure of upcoming touches for both partners.

In all cases, there must be mutual consent, either expressed or implied, to touching the genital areas by both partners. We can express consent by taking the partner's hand and placing it on our genitals. Or we can communicate consent and interest by making the genitals easily accessible.

Touching the face and kissing the lips and breasts are very important preliminary steps to prepare both partners for genital touching. These preliminary touches are generally sufficient to cause moistening of the vagina and erection of the penis. The fluids in the moistened vagina are not always equally distributed throughout the opening and the canal; fluids tend to settle in the bottom of the canal. The female organ that is the most sensitive, the clitoris, is dependent on vaginal fluids to reduce friction of stroking and caressing. To assure that moisture is covering the clitoris, the loving partner may wish to take the fluid from the lower part of the canal and spread it on the clitoris or clitoral hood. Inserting a finger into the vagina and moving it across the top of the vaginal opening will moisten the clitoris. Moistened, the clitoris is more sensitive to strokes by the partner's hand. Some women prefer light rotary motion, and others prefer an up-and-down motion, simulating a penis. As the pleasure grows, there may be a need to alter the stroking. The speed of the movement may be increased or decreased. A loving mate may wish to use two fingers. Feeling the up-and-down motion of one finger on each side of the clitoris can be an exciting experience for many women. It is most important to the male partner to have assurance from his mate that touches to and around the inside of the vagina are pleasure giving and not a cause for discomfort.

Loving touches to the inside of the vagina begin with much care, the intention to express tenderness and joy, and the desire to give pleasure. Previous touches, such as kissing the lips and fondling the breasts, bring about the "sexual arousal" associated with lubrication of the vagina. Direct touches or attempts to penetrate the vagina prior to arousing these good feelings can cause pain instead of pleasure. Caring lovers learn that caresses to other parts of the body must precede vaginal touching. A finger may be inserted with ease once the vaginal walls are moistened. At first a slow and careful penetration is made by pressing the finger into the canal opening. A slow back-and-forth motion will help moisten the finger and allow it to enter the opening more comfortably. Once the finger is comfortably inside the vagina, an exploration for additional pleasure may begin. The inner lining has many folds and varying formations. Touches to the area directly behind the clitoris are also greatly pleasurable for many women. The opening to the urinary track is in this area, and light-fingered touches can stimulate many women to greater pleasure. If the vaginal opening feels wide enough to accept it comfortably, introducing a second finger may heighten the stimulation. If the two fingers enter the vagina simultaneously and with ease, it is possible that the woman is approaching readiness for intercourse; however, additional touches from the two fingers may be welcome before assuming a coital position. One may use fingers to simulate the in-and-out motions produced by a penis. They may be curved to touch the upper front walls of the vagina in a rotation stroking manner or in squeezing, cupped manner. This area of the vagina is rarely stimulated in intercourse and can provide additional pleasure. The female may indicate her pleasure by moving her pelvic area. Simultaneously moving the thumb across the clitoris while caressing the inside of the vagina can create further excitement. This latter combination of loving touches may indeed be so stimulating as to lead to climax without penile penetration. Some women express a preference for experiencing an orgasm in this manner, whereas others consider the touches preparatory to the entry of the penis.

Loving touches to the male partner's genitals can also be very rewarding. They bring about more responsive sentiments and good feelings than many women realize. Because our culture has allowed us to think and act as if males were the active touchers and females the passive receivers of sexual touches, many women have overlooked the opportunity to use affectionate genital touching as a sign of caring and endearment. Touching the male's pubic hair is a pleasant way to begin caressing the genitals. A female can demonstrate warmth and caring simply by touching, stroking, or lightly patting the pubic area of her mate. Most males welcome female touches in which there is a gentle movement of the fingertips across the hair leading down to the penile shaft. Such touches express a desire for sexual intimacy. For most men, the base of the penile shaft is a sexually sensitive area where delicate female touches are welcome. The skin at the base of the penis is joined by the scrotum sac on the lower side and protrudes out from the pubic area on the upper side. Thus, a clasping hand around the base of the penis will come in contact with the corrugations of the scrotum on one side and the pubic hair on the other side. Particularly for males who do not experience direct vaginal contact with this portion of the penile shaft, the manual touching of this area, outside of coitus, is highly pleasing. Most men enjoy having the penile shaft stimulated by their partner, encircling the shaft in the hand and touching the skin covering the urinary tract (urethra) on the lower side of the penis. The loving mate may trace the urinary tract from the base to the tip of the penis while pressing in on it gently. Touching the crown of the penis (the rounded portion near the top of the shaft) continues to increase sexual excitement and the joy of being loved. Assuming that previous touches have aroused the man, the urinary opening at the top of the shaft provides lubricating fluids that may be moved pleasurably across the head and around the crown of the penis. The lubricating fluids may also be moved down and around the penile shaft, allowing the curved hand to move with ease over the slippery, hardened penis. This experience prepares the man to penetrate the vagina easily, and it heightens the pleasure of both partners.

Caressing exploration of the male's scrotum is a great source of pleasure for both partners. Touching this area requires a keen awareness of a mate's reactions; too much pressure may cause pain. Light, delicate pressure, applied with fingertips or cupped hands, can demonstrate intimate caring, an assurance of love and sexual desire. The female partner can vary her mate's pleasure by delicately fingering the highly sensitive skin of the scrotum. One variation is to cup one testicle in the hand, encompassing and caressing it. Another is to squeeze the scrotum sac lightly. The light squeeze may be given by placing one finger on one side of the sac and another on the opposite side, then bringing them together, with different portions of the sac remaining in between the two fingers. When both partners exhibit an openness and willingness to engage in touching and verbal interaction in a reciprocal manner, their most rewarding experiences will occur.

## Sharing Orgasm

Without our sense of touch, most of us would not be able to enjoy the pleasure of orgasm. Most of us experience our first orgasms through self-arousal. People can benefit greatly from exploring their own bodies; self-touching for greater self-awareness was described in Chapter 5. It is not uncommon for a lack of understanding about the feelings and responses of our mate to hamper our lovemaking seriously. Many of us feel shy or otherwise unable to tell a sexual partner how we feel about the touches he or she gives to bring us to orgasm. Many men assume that their love mates are pleased with the touchings they receive. However, a substantial number of women do not experience the gratification that men imagine. Too often, the woman's pleasure is limited to an awareness that she is able to gratify her man; the woman's excitement, then, comes less from the sensations of the man's touch and more from seeing his excitement. Under these conditions, many women feel that they are simply the vehicle for the sexual aggressions of men; it is unfortunate that so many women fall into this stereotyped role in which their own feelings seem unimportant. Consequently, many women do not initiate or fully enjoy sexual experiences. They often feel that imitiating the gestures may be considered too aggressive and possibly threatening.

Unfortunately, most males in our society misunderstand the reactions they create in the women they touch. Although they might intend to express love and sexual desires, many seem only to clutch and grab. Their touches, ironically, lessen their mate's interest in intimacy instead of increasing it. But the woman commonly persists in her passivity, hinting nothing of her frustration. She fears puncturing her mate's ego by criticizing his "performance" in bed. Clearly, the man's drive to do the touching, as great as it may be, is not a measurement or a guarantee of his mate's satisfaction. Although he may feel that his touches are irresistible, his mate may have only a lukewarm, if not a negative, response.

In such a relationship, it is likely that there is a parallel lack of understanding by the woman. Many women do not understand their mate's intentions in making love; they may fail to perceive a sincere desire to please them with caresses. In addition, many women are ignorant of the male cycle of arousal and climax, including the fact that a man can experience a decrease and resurgence of an erection several times during lovemaking before ejaculation. Indeed, many men are themselves unaware that an erection can "wax and wane" several times in a sexual encounter.

Both male and female partners, then, can experience a lack of understanding of the dynamics of their sexual relations. This state of ignorance has a seriously limiting effect on their enjoyment. To avoid such a limitation, we must each take the responsibility of becoming aware of our own sexual feelings. Once we understand our own preferences, communicating them to a mate is a vital part of achieving a rewarding sexual relationship. The willingness to share with a loving partner the knowledge of one's own unique responses to genital touching can greatly enhance the sense of love and intimacy. It implies that we deeply trust the mate and believe that he or she truly cares about our innermost feelings.

In order to achieve a better understanding of each other's sexual feelings and to explore new possibilities for enjoyment together, a couple may devote some time to caressing each other's body in a comfortable setting. One element crucial to a comfortable setting is privacy. Both partners should feel confident that there will be no interruptions. Without pressure of time, the partners can caress each other's nude body reciprocally. The goal should not be to reach orgasm but to feel free in lovingly touching each other for long periods of time (twenty to thirty minutes). Later, they might share verbally what it felt like to touch and be touched. The discussion is not for sexual arousal, but simply a means of communicating intimately with one's mate. It is a reaffirmation of trust and the willingness to share one's feelings openly.

Entering full coitus (with the penis in the vagina) is perhaps the most profound sharing of touch in a loving exchange. The vagina becomes moist and dilated, ready to receive the penis. The engorged penis has become erect. The vagina accepts the penis, drawing it into its warm, soothing depth; the penis easily penetrates the vagina. There is a beauty in union, a joy of fulfillment between lovers.

Each of us is unique in our response to sexual touching. We are distinctively different in how we feel and think about sexual touches. Our responses are a culmination of previous physical interactions with others. If we have felt loved in cuddling situations not involving sex activity previously, we are most likely to feel loved in cuddling associated with coitus. We all adjust to our mates in unique ways. If we were noncuddlers, we will probably seek out coital positions that are not confining but leave us relatively free to express ourselves in movement. To be fully loving, we must be able to share our uniqueness, our creativity, in intercourse. Each partner will relate to the other in his or her own style. Preferred touching positions (descriptions abound in sex manuals and magazines) will affect our approach. A heavy-set lover would not want to "crush" a tiny mate. An unusually tall mate would approach a shorter lover in a manner considerate of their differences. A multitude of positions, although erotically interesting to fantasize and worthy of experimentation, may not actually be more pleasurable in practice. Positions may become secondary in sexual touching in comparison to the expressive intent and emotional relatedness involved in the exchange. Thus our expression of love and caring, our commitment to pleasing and sharing, our communication and warmth, our joy of giving and receiving are the components that allow sexual touching to fulfill us. They can put sexual touching among the peak experiences that enrich our lives.

In the United States, adult sex-touching is increasing. The Masters and Johnson report suggests that there is more variety in marital touching and a greater incidence of premarital and extramarital sex. The last decade saw an increase in the numbers of books and movies explaining and demonstrating techniques in sex-touching. The sexual revolution of the seventies has created an atmosphere in which our awareness of capabilities for touch involved in the sex act have been fully explored. There are probably no modes of sex-touching that have not been detailed in the literature or the movies. But noticeable by its absence from the wide range of sex exploration is the affective component that accompanies such touching. We still need to understand and describe better what happens to us emotionally, and perhaps spiritually, as we engage in the sex act. Touching that is not just a "tactical measure" but an expression of sincere love can help us improve the transmission of meaning in lovemaking.

# chapter nine

# Touching for Happiness and Health

## Happiness Is . . . a Touch

How do we attain happiness for ourselves and help others attain it? Our lives might be much more rewarding, bound by fewer conflicts, and filled with greater pleasure if we could go to a well of happiness, draw a bucketful, and give it to our friends every time they show signs of needing some. We might even draw an extra bucket or two to have on hand, for ourselves, for those occasions when our personal supply runs low. Characteristically, happiness is not a substance or product that we can take at will from one location, store in another place, and draw upon at another time. For a writer, happiness might be finding the right word at the right time. For a distraught friend, happiness might be the right touch applied appropriately at the right time. In both cases a need is fulfilled, and when it is fulfilled, the accompanying feeling is one of happiness. Thus, happiness is not a state or quality that we can pursue directly in and of itself; it is a by-product, one that results from the fulfillment of that which was desired or needed. The greater the fulfillment, the greater the happiness. Thus we might conclude that happiness is an affective state of contentment that is attained through fulfillment of a need. Touching exchanges in themselves cannot always bring happiness . . . but they sure can help. In our search for being happily alive, we need touching's nourishment just as we need stimulation of the senses of sight, hearing, taste, and smell (Masters and Johnson 1972).

Imagine our lives without the sense of touch! We might be able to function in a limited manner without the other senses, but we would find it difficult, if not impossible, to function without touch. It is through touching that we are able to fulfill a large share of our human needs and, in doing so, to attain happiness. Helen Keller told how touching became a source of happiness for her. She reported how it brought the outside world into her isolation. After learning to communicate with her tutor through touching signals, she reported her joy enthusiastically, saying: "Paradise is attained by touch" (Lobsenz 1970).

## Touching in the Hierarchy of Human Needs

According to Abraham Maslow's theory of self-actualization, there are six levels of human needs that must be satisfied for our fulfillment as persons (Kalish 1967). We tend to seek the satisfaction of higher-level needs only when those at lower levels have been satisfied. Touching can play a vital role in the satisfaction of these various levels of needs.

*Survival.* At the first level of Maslow's hierarchy are minimal survival needs, such as food, air, water, and habitable temperature. With the aid of our sense of touch, we can achieve what we need to survive. As infants, we seek to touch the mother's breast to fulfill our need for food. This tactual activity leads to satisfaction of hunger and brings us contentment. Throughout life, we need to relieve the touching pressure in our bladder and bowels to satisfy our need for elimination. The warmth and heat from an open fire when our hands are "frozen" is a source of happiness. The coolness of a dip in the pool on a hot summer afternoon is pleasing. The list grows: the touch of water to parched lips, the touch of bread to the mouth of a hungry person; the touch of a firm bed after an exhausting day. All of these tactual experiences bring us happiness by fulfilling our most basic survival needs.

*Stimulation.* Level two of Maslow's hierarchy of needs is the need for stimulation. We have a natural motivation toward and an innate need for the stimulation we can receive from sexual experiences, novelty seeking, manipulation for learning and exploring, or any type of activity.

The need for sexual stimulation is one of the most predominant needs we have. Although the other senses spark our desire for sexual stimulation, it is primarily through touch that we satisfy this need. Sexual satisfaction depends upon our ability to express ourselves through a great variety of tender touching modes applied to our own bodies or to that of our partner.

Critical to the satisfaction of the need for sexual stimulation is our ability to learn. Unlike the need for air and rest, which are satisfied without learning, sexual needs require learned behavior to be satisfied. We must learn to touch ourselves and our love mates in appropriate ways that lead to a pleasure-filled sense of satisfaction.

Appropriate, natural, and self-rewarding sexual touching abounds in individuals who (1) have no guilt feelings about sexual expression, (2) have strong needs for affection, and (3) demonstrate a sexually noncallous feeling toward others. The prospect of feeling guilty is one of the common reasons why we avoid fulfilling our need for sexual stimulation. If our conscious or internalized values signal us to refrain from sexual expression when we feel a desire for it, we will experience a conflict between our needs and their satisfaction. If we have a very strong association between the sex act and guilt, we will probably hesitate until the circumstances are "right". Because of the high incidence of touching in the sex act, guilt feelings about sex are often transferred and generalized to a simple guilt feeling about any type of interpersonal touching, even though the touching is not directed toward the sex act. Fortunately, people who have satisfactorily "worked out" their guilt feelings regarding sexual expressions tend to have equal success with their feelings toward other types of touching.

In addition to the need for sexual activity, Maslow's concept of level two—the need for stimulation—also includes exploration, manipulation, and novelty. A lack of activity tends to produce fatigue, apathy, and boredom. Thus, our contacts with the outside world through touch are important to mental health. As children, we sought to explore our environment tactually, to touch objects with our hands, even to manipulate objects with our tongues. Any new object or person became a target of tactual exploration because of our attraction to *novelty*. We discarded old toys and touched new ones to manipulate them, to have the feeling of control over them—that is, until we tired of the process and sought other novelties for touching and exploring.

Even as adults, we find happiness in tactual exploration and manipulation. Many of us derive great joy and satisfaction from knitting, handcrafts, woodworking, playing a musical instrument, or tinkering with some type of equipment or machinery.

*Security Needs.*  Safety, security, and protection are at the third level of the hierarchy of needs. In our earliest years, we had these needs fulfilled through the care of our parents and other significant persons. Our parents held us in the safety and security of their arms when we were frightened. They grabbed us or pulled us out of the path of cars and other potential dangers. They held our hands when we first attempted to climb stairs or cross streets.

**129**

They held us when we first ventured into the ocean or a swimming pool. They tucked us securely into bed at night. These touches gave us the foundation for feeling safe and secure.

As we matured from infancy to adolescence, we sought out and continued to fulfill our needs for safety; we selected, touched, and interacted with friends whose actions, words, and deeds reaffirmed our feelings of security. Even as adults, we continue to use touching to satisfy our need for safety and security. We like to hold onto something or someone when the path on which we walk looks precarious. Even some of us who think we are self-sufficient reach out to grab the person who is closest when a sudden danger appears. In old age, when we begin to lose some of our physical strength, sure footing, and sense of self-sufficiency, we may rely more heavily upon touch for our sense of security. In one way or another, we tend to use touch whenever we need it for a sense of safety and security throughout our lives.

*Needs for Belonging, Closeness, and Love.*   At the fourth level of Maslow's hierarchy of needs is the need for belonging and closeness. These characteristics of interpersonal relationships can be communicated through touch and are reciprocal. If we move to belong, chances are we will belong; if we offer our closeness, we have a great chance for being close. However, in seeking satisfaction of these needs, we do risk possible rejection. If this occurs and there are repeated rejections, we can become very skeptical about further interpersonal risk taking. Then isolation and alienation results in a feeling of emptiness and lack of fulfillment.

On the other hand, a relationship of belonging and closeness is invariably linked with a high incidence of interpersonal touching. Touching exchanges are both an effective way to attain such a relationship and the natural expression of it.

The need for affection and love is also associated with the fourth level of Maslow's hierarchy. More than any other need, our desire to love and be loved prompts us to enter touching exchanges. If we feel unloved, we tend to feel unhappy. A measurement of the feeling of being loved is the amount of loving touches we receive from significant others. We depend greatly upon touch as a means of communicating love. If we are cuddled, hugged, or gently held, we feel loved. If we are hugged frequently, we feel that we are valued and loved more profoundly. This beautiful sense of feeling loved is one of our greatest sources of happiness. If this love is removed, we feel lost and unhappy until we regain a sense of being loved by someone. That sense of being loved by some-one—whether we are infant, child, teenager, or adult—is accom-panied by loving touches and allows us to be happy. Some of us have stronger needs for affection and love than others, and our in-dividual needs occasionally fluctuate. When our morale is a little low, when we feel like "no one understands us," when we feel alone and neglected, we can usually regain our equilibrium if we receive some TLT's (Tender Loving Touches).

Without our sense of touch, we would be without the pro-found rewards that intimacy brings (Masters and Johnson, 1972). Our happiness in human relatedness would not exist if we could not touch another human being. If we could not share our tactual selves with others, our world would be very bleak and would offer little hope for the fellowship that enriches our lives. Some persons have a tremendous need to be loved that they are unable to fulfill for some reason. A case in point is a young woman who was very unhappy with her life. She consistently sought ways to do away with her life, either by taking overdoses of sleeping pills or by slashing her wrists. Having been sexually molested as a child, she rejected and expressed mistrust of all touching gestures from both men and women. A young man with much patience and perseverance sought out her companionship. After much verbal exploration, they identified the cause of her mistrust in touch ex-changes. Gradually she learned to welcome friendly reciprocal touching exchanges, which she then reported brought her the greatest happiness she'd ever known. Radically changed, she grew to value herself and ceased making threats of suicide. She decided: "I want to live, to touch, and be touched in a loving way.

**131**

Giving and receiving loving touches, not just for sex only, but for caring, for endearment, is what makes my life meaningful. I want to be around for a long time so I can happily continue to do it."

*Esteem.* At the fifth level of Maslow's hierarchy of needs are esteem and self-esteem. These two needs call for gaining the respect of others and achieving and maintaining respect for ourselves. We can demonstrate our esteem in a nonverbal way with light pats on the back to friends who need encouragement or when we wish to give praise. Even light touches to the forearms or shoulders convey recognition and high regard.

Not being esteemed, particularly not being esteemed by individuals we regard highly, detracts from our happiness. When we fail to receive a greeting or salutation from those we esteem or love, our contentment falters, and we begin to imagine reasons for being slighted. A simple touch on the shoulder or a handshake can restore or maintain our ease and contentment. As children, many of us have experienced lack of attention and lack of recognition. An only child, for example, suddenly faces the reality that a new child will be entering the household and competing for recognition. The new child appears to garner all the recognition, to the sibling's dismay. Parents can help to dispel the older child's worries and provide reassurance simply by giving extra hugs and cuddling that show special recognition and esteem.

*Self-actualization.* On the sixth and top level of human needs, according to Maslow, is self-actualization. Satisfaction of this need suggests that we are utilizing our talents and abilities to the maximum. The goal here is one of reaching our fullest potential. It implies that we achieved fulfillment of the needs outlined in levels one through five. In reaching this level, we maximize our potential for using touch as a valuable tool in the attainment of happiness.

*Happiness Is Personal and Unique.* Effects of touching as they relate to happiness are not always predictable. Some types of touching may bring happiness to one person while they annoy another. Many children, for instance, seek out cuddling, but there are others who avoid it at all costs. The attitude toward touching that one develops in early childhood is often carried over into adulthood. Some people are like the individual who explains: "I feel happy when I am loose and free. I am the happiest when I get up real early on a cold morning, go to the beach, and find that I am the only one there. I let myself go because I am free. When my feet touch the cool sand and I run across the beach, the cold winds hitting my face and body, it's so invigorating. It's like being in touch with nature, in contact with God." Another individual relates touching and happiness to the realization of contact with family members. To her, a closeness must exist for her to feel fulfilled. The closeness can be gained either through actual touching and holding or by just being nearby. "It is something like loving God," she explains. "By touching people in a loving and caring way, it seems to me that we are 'touching' God, and that is when we are our happiest."

Happiness is undoubtedly an individual thing. No one can make us happy. In a way, we choose to be happy by focusing on certain basic needs or goals, the attainment of which we determine is required for happiness. By setting our hearts on things we can achieve reasonably well and then setting out to do so, we create our own happiness. Our resources for touching and being touched are among the most natural and vital means for satisfying our needs and gaining happiness.

## Healing Touches

We can also use touch to promote health. In fact, touch in itself can sometimes bring healing—physical, psychological, and spiritual.

*Massage.* In infancy we receive the benefit of massage as we are bathed, oiled, powdered, and generally fussed over.

**133**

Strokes to the scalp, arms, legs, and buttocks that clean and soothe us also stimulate the circulatory system and leave us with a sense of contentment.

Of course, the opportunity to receive the benefits of massage decreases drastically when we move into late childhood and adolescence. We take over the job ourselves and tend to neglect certain areas, such as our backs, necks, ears, and genitals. These areas are cleaned with little enthusiasm and consequently receive less massaging stimulation.

Too few of us attempt to regain the pleasure that can be derived from massage. Frequently, we wait for illness or severe fatigue before we consider treating ourselves to the relief of massage. Elizabeth, a woman in San Francisco, sought out a professional massage to improve a sore leg muscle. In the process, she agreed to a complete body massage. Her reaction follows: "The touching, the massaging of my whole body gave me a sense of contentment I have not experienced since I was last bathed as a small girl by my mother. The massage stimulates muscle and skin areas on my body which I think I had forgotten were part of me. I felt as happy and content as a little baby." In her enthusiasm, Elizabeth convinced a straightlaced friend to try the same. The friend found that the massage left her with a glow of happiness and a feeling of being "reborn."

The experience of these women holds a lesson for us, but it need not imply that we should seek a professional masseuse. Each of us can give a body massage to a mate or other loved ones. A couple in St. Louis discovered the relaxing and "healing" effect of massage and began giving each of their two children, ages five and seven, a bedtime bath followed by a massage at least once a week. After the children were asleep, they gave each other the same soothing treatment. Massage increases circulation throughout the body, reducing the carbon dioxide in our tissues; it is the carbon dioxide that creates the feeling of tiredness and lack of ease. The greater sense of well-being we receive from massage is thus a physical phenomenon. Because of the close

**134**

association between our physical and psychological selves, massage can also affect us emotionally, reducing our anxiety and evoking a sense of renewed vitality and fresh perspective. Especially for sexual partners, the experience is enhanced by the psychological closeness and intimacy it creates.

*Touching of the Sick.* The Anointing of the Sick is a religious ritual intended to bring spiritual and sometimes physical or psychological healing. In this rite, the sick person is touched and lightly rubbed with consecrated oils symbolic of healing. The officiating person touches the body of the ill person—possibly the hands, feet, head, and all the sense organs (eyes, ears, nose and tongue)—with oil and evokes the faith of all in attendance in a prayer for healing. Today, therapeutic touch for healing is becoming a widespread practice. What was once considered, at best, miraculous and, at worst, quackery is now accepted as the natural transfer of energy from one body to another. Touch-healers, it is said, "spark" the latent energy of the ill, and researchers claim that the "power to heal" lies in many of us (Krieger 1975). We need only exercise it. For some people, this power to heal through touch is also connected to religious faith, as in early Christianity, to bring about miracle cures.

Touch-healers, including doctors, nurses, and religious persons, must commit themselves unselfishly to the needs of the subject and concentrate on passing their energies in his or her direction. They scan the body of the infirm, and through an unusual extrasensory perception, they locate the malady; while the subject remains passive, the healer searches. The process appears mystically frightening—to transfer our individual life force to another person and effect a cure. Although they cannot analyze yesterday's cures, scientists say that today's "touch treatments" restore energy, reduce anxiety, control blood pressure, and modify body temperature. The evidence is so convincing that courses in the healing power of hands are offered to nurses throughout the United States.

Each trainee healer in therapeutic touch is cautioned that the art of healing is demanding and that immediate results cannot be expected. They learn that the patients' perception of the illness and their anticipation of recovery are significant factors, perhaps more significant than their belief in the benefits of therapeutic touch. Trainees also learn that the unskilled use of therapeutic touch may allow energy to enter the patients too quickly, giving them a drained feeling and sometimes causing pain.

Therapeutic touch enthusiasts make broad claims. They suggest, for instance, that we can learn to heal ourselves through practice. A St. Louis nursing home administrator claims that he has been able to use therapeutic touch on himself to ward off flu and colds. Others claim that therapeutic touch eliminates or reduces menstrual cramps and controls bloat. Director of Nurses, Carol Lloyd, reports that patients at Oak Knoll Nursing Home in St. Louis were able to reduce their intake of tranquilizers by 75 percent through therapeutic touch. According to Karol White (1979), therapeutic touch has lowered body temperature (in the presence of virus colds, sore throats, flu, and the like), reduced swelling (for fractures and sprains), stopped bleeding, and eased pain. It is especially successful in eliminating lung congestion, reducing phantom-limb pain following amputation, and reducing diabetics' dependence on insulin. White explains that her own treatment reduced anxiety and lowered her voice tone about four levels; moreover, it changed her breathing—making it slower, deeper, and easier. Her skin color grew rosy—a direct result, reports White, of more efficient breathing and greater oxygen supply.

The use of therapeutic touch with hospital patients has been extensively studied by Dolores Krieger (1975, 1976). She identified a group of volunteers and evaluated the effects of touch on their hemoglobin (red blood cell) counts. She found an increase in red blood cells in response to therapeutic touch; this phenomenon creates an increase in the vital oxygen content, so important for cell growth and healing. One patient was given short periods of touch within an eighteen hour period for treatment of nervous exhaustion. The patient's hemoglobin values increased from 9.4 to 10.9. Another patient, suffering from an endocrine imbalance, was given therapeutic touch in short periods. Her hemoglobin values increased from 14.1 to 14.9 during a six-hour period. Another patient, admitted for cataract surgery, entered the hospital with a hemoglobin value of 14.1. Shortly after receiving therapeutic touch, his count rose to 15.6. One of the most spectacular cases was that of a corporate vice-president suffering from nervous exhaustion. Over a forty-five-minute period, he was given several short touch treatments that were correlated to a hemoglobin value increase from 12.5 to 14.1.

To the scientist, then, therapeutic touch brings observable and desirable phenomena. The results may be anticipated and measured, if not completely controlled. To the patient, therapeutic touch offers a possible source of relief that can no longer be considered the ministerings of a quack. Today, surprising facts are emerging about the significance of touch and the wide variety of healing powers we have in our hands.

# chapter ten

# Let's Start Touching: Here's How to Do It

Let's begin a rewarding touching program by taking an inventory of our current touching activities. Stop and think for a moment about the routine of your day. How many people do you touch? Can you picture them? Have you considered why you touch them? Mull these questions over before you continue reading. If you are like the average American, you probably don't touch too many people during the course of a day. Chances are that you do not have a high incidence of touching to express concern, care, nurturance, sympathy, empathy, or friendship.

Now bring to mind once again the various people you meet in the course of a day. Would you like to improve your use of touch in relating to any of them? Which ones? In this chapter, we consider some alternative ways of using touch more deliberately and effectively in interpersonal relationships of various kinds—including relationships with one's mate, young children, teenagers, older adults, acquaintances, colleagues, and close friends of either sex. But first we summarize some general guidelines for the adoption of new touching behaviors.

## General Guidelines

Because of the high potential for misinterpreting different forms of touching in our culture, it is to our advantage to learn some rules. If we follow some appropriate, common-sense guidelines, we can make positive changes in our behavior. Our behavior will no longer be determined by the society's unwritten rules that gest that touching is the exclusive domain of combat or sexual activity. We can succeed in converting ourselves from nontouchers to touchers, or from touchers to better touchers.

1. Touching, to be effective and rewarding, must be undertaken at appropriate times and places. We must learn to perceive the right time. A touch given at the wrong time can cause frustration and even lead to distress. Giving out a touch indicating sexual interest when the time and occasion call for a consoling touch will only confuse the recipient and assist in building up resentment about all touching activities. On the other hand, on an occasion when congratulations are in order, a person might be ready to receive an embrace, possibly would even expect one; the time is right to express recognition and share joy through a hug.

The place is also important. A football player patting the buttocks of a fellow player while fully clothed in an open field is acceptable in our society. The same act in an empty locker room is not equally acceptable.

2. Touching becomes effective when others are receptive to contact. We must learn to be sensitive to the readiness of others to be touched. Because of temperament and former experience, many people are skeptical about almost any touch, especially if it

is from an unknown person. We must not let our enthusiasm for touching blind us to other people's feelings; if we do, our good intentions could evoke outright rejection. We should begin a new touching program by first developing an awareness of the preferences of people around us. We can test a person's reaction to invasion of their private space by observing what happens as we move closer. If the person starts to back away as we continue to draw closer, we know we have penetrated the individual's space bubble; we can deduce that the person would most likely feel some discomfort with more than the ordinary handshake.

**3.** As with any behavior, a touching behavior pattern becomes more effective and meaningful when we communicate our intent prior to undertaking unexpected actions. We frequently use nonverbal cues to indicate an imminent touch. Puckered lips tell that a kiss is on its way, and a fist indicates that a punch can be expected.

Prior notification can reduce much anxiety and is similar to the notification and explanation we receive from doctors and dentists before they touch us in certain clinical ways. We can simply tell people that we wish to expand our sense of communication through touching. They might react with a number of questions, but they shouldn't be too shocked the next time they are given a literal pat on the back for a job well done.

Explanations of changes of behavior, even for the simplest acts of touching, are vital to the success of a change in touching patterns in relation to persons who know us well. Our simplest acts of touching, once established with friends and associates, become an expected ritual. If we modify the ritual in any minor way or replace it by another, we can best do so by advising people beforehand that we plan to make a change. If, for example, we wish to replace the ordinary greeting handshake with a more warmhearted hug and embrace, we should let our associates know beforehand. Giving friends a big hug and embrace (when we have been the handshaker type) without telling them beforehand that we simply intend it to be a more profound greeting may generate some confusion or question. We should inform friends of any unexpected change in our method of greeting or relating to avoid misinterpretation. An effort to change our behavior will be effective if not only we ourselves but also our close associates feel comfortable with it.

**4.** Be sincere and consistent with touching communication. Successful touching requires that we personally identify the intended meaning and touch only with this intent. Touch interactions can have disguised intentions and result in confused messages and resentment. It is very easy to deceive ourselves in this matter.

If we feel lonely or crave attention, we should not satisfy our need by feigning some other message such as sympathy, congratulations, or protectiveness. The recipient of such a touch can sense the discrepancy, perhaps without being able to identify it, and may react negatively. Such behavior is self-defeating, because in the long run, it does not lead to fulfillment of our actual need.

**5.** Touching should be used primarily for communicating positive feelings. When touching is used to place hidden demands, expectations, or control on someone, a negative reaction generally results. The negative reaction may be expressed in any number of ways—varying from ignoring to resentment, refusal to comply, rejection, anger, or outright rebellion. The total experience becomes an unwholesome one for both toucher and receiver, because it perverts the concept of touch as a means of improving and enjoying relationships and destroys openness and trust.

A common misuse of touching is to demand or control within

the sex act. Recipients of sexually demanding or controlling touches feel used, abused, and often degraded, perceiving themselves as objects—not unique, esteemed individuals.

Another misuse of touch occurs in relationships with children. Touch is used in many ways with children—to express affection, approval, disapproval, restraint, commands, punishment, and so on. The negative effect comes in when seeming expressions of love and affection are used to trick a child into compliance, or when affection is withheld as a means of control. Children can detect such tactics and are hurt by the sense of being unloved.

**6.** If we are to engage in close tactual contact with others, we must be well groomed enough to make the experience pleasant for those we touch. There is nothing like dirty hands, dirty fingernails, greasy hair, prickly whiskers, worn-out deodorant, or unclean clothing to thwart the effect of a touching gesture. In addition, we should view self-care as an appropriate way of loving and respecting ourselves. Besides its pragmatic purpose, the self-touching we do as part of grooming should bring us a sense of well-being and confidence that we can carry over to our relationships with others.

Now that we have reviewed some general do's and don't for adopting new touching behaviors, let us consider some ways to begin in everyday relationships. You may have a relationship with a specific person in mind or several different relationships. It's up to you.

## Our Mates

Let's reflect a routine morning for many Americans. Most of us are not too verbal early in the day. Our speaking facilities' low ebb discourages us from entering into verbal communication. Some people are unable, or at least unwilling, to communicate at all early in the morning. Thus, morning is a good time to put nonverbal skills into action, particularly the nonverbal skill of touching. This is an opportune time to reach out and give a recognition touch to that significant person in our lives—our mate. This gesture will enhance the interpersonal relationship and communication. An affectionate greeting from a loved one, even before arising, assures us of our bond and reminds us that we are loved. It bridges the separateness we sometimes feel.

Why not start tomorrow morning! Great boldness is not necessary. Go over (or roll over); get next to him or her, and give a tender recognition touch. A light squeeze of the hand, a caress on the forehead, or a stroke under the chin suffices. Reaching out and briefly holding or patting hands can be a reassuring gesture with which to start the day. Pressing the fingers and palms lightly and holding them for just a few seconds can communicate a loving greeting that is not easily verbalized. This communication reaches the soul. The intent of the touch must always be transmitted; the sender has to intend in a positive sense to communicate a greeting or warm message. When the sender intends to communicate something else, the message will be confused. If the sender is angry or has negative feelings about the intent, the communication will falter. If the loved one inquires about this nonverbal message later, we can explain that the intent was to express recognition and confirmation of his or her value to us as a person.

Assuming that our partner is so inclined, we may even want to start the day in a profoundly loving way through sex. A mutual interest in entering into a love-touching exchange might begin as the morning greeting changes from a patting to a stroking gesture. We may communicate this desire by taking the mate's hand within our own and guiding it to the breast or chest or lowering it smoothly over the stomach and down to the genitals.

Morning departures are good times for loving mates to touch to reinforce their commitment and relay messages of caring and mutual support. This doesn't necessarily mean a passionate kiss at the doorstep each morning. A simple touch, a light kiss, is often enough to convey the message. The hug expresses togetherness and communicates a sense of belonging as well as reassurance. Such a gesture is a tremendous boost as we set out to face the challenges and problems of the day.

Reunion at the close of a busy day is a natural occasion for communicating through touch. Those beautiful evenings when we are feeling great about the day, particularly when everything seemed to go right, are best for communicating openly and freely. Touch messages for these occasions are happy hugs, reinforced with verbalization that explains the reason for our joy. We can also enjoy a full spin or two, effectively making a closing gesture of holding hands; this is a rewarding tactual communication for that significant person in our lives.

After a frustrating day of conflicts, problems, or unrewarding work, we need consoling hugs or caresses. If we try to be sensitive to mood, we can generally determine the right time to approach a mate with a soothing touch or a light massage on the shoulders or neck. Such touches help to minimize anguish, fear, and frustration.

Bedtime is an excellent time to enjoy loving touches. Our bodies and minds decelerate, and our abilities for verbalization are reduced; the affective side of the brain is more open to nonverbal communication. Particularly for those of us with children, it may be just about the only time for lovemaking.

A little fun and humor can bring variety and new life to a sexual relationship. Tickling is potentially fun-giving, perhaps the most fun of touching exchanges. We need only reflect upon our childhood activities to bring some of those tickling techniques to mind. Most areas of the body are susceptible to tickling; for most people, the most sensitive areas are under the arms, the bottom of the feet, and around the neck. Tickling is a very delicate touching action. The tickler must be aware of changing feedback from the "ticklee" and stop short of excessive contact. At certain levels, tickling can cease to be pleasant and may even become painful.

Unfortunately, when we become adults, we think of tickling as childish and discard the idea of such playful activities. If we want to, we can still have enough childlike qualities in our personalities to appreciate this type of touching. Why not try a tickling exchange game with a loving mate? Attempt to find the areas of his or her body that respond to tickling, and determine which touches produce the most pleasure without creating discomfort, starting slowly at first and letting the exchange last only a few seconds. An excessive or discomforting exchange might discourage future exchanges. Used in moderation, tickling communicates mutual fun that can only enhance an interpersonal relationship with a mate.

There are many other ways to bring fun, teasing, and humor into a sexual relationship. One of these is pinching a sensitive area, particularly the buttocks. Both men and women can give this a try. It is important to make sure that the meaning of the pinch is clear. It might be a teasing, complimentary, or suggestive gesture or some combination of the three. The trick is to make sure it is fun for both partners; an accompanying verbal communication may help clarify the intent.

Variety helps keep lovemaking interesting and alive. It takes some creativity and willingness to experiment to maximize enjoyment of sexual relating. One form of body-to-body contact that can provide some variety is licking. This highly sensuous act is accompanied by the added sensation of moisture. The tongue may easily be used in a side-to-side, up-and-down, or circular motion as it is brought into contact with the lips, face, ear lobe, or genitals. The tip of the tongue may be held in a flattened position or a pointed tip to give finer licking strokes. Another variation in lovemaking is nibbling. Ear lobes, nipples, or even fingertips make good spots for nibbling, for both men and women.

Of course, kissing and caressing hold unlimited possibilities for creative lovemaking. There are as many places to kiss and caress as there are parts of the body. And there are innumerable modes of kissing or caressing. A little ingenuity and daring, coupled with sensitivity to a partner's preferences, can show a mate that we really care about him or her; we care enough to put some extra thought into the relationship.

If you've never tried it before, you may want to experiment with kissing the feet of your loving mate. For many people, kissing the sensitive sides and arches of the feet with closed lips creates a delightfully erotic sensation.

We all have evenings when the whole body aches, when we feel so dead tired that we aren't quite up to the experience of coitus. Some alternative ways of showing love on such occasions are the full body massage, sharing a warm bath or shower, or some combination of these.

If you have never taken turns at massage with your mate, you really must try it. You can gear it to your mate's readiness and taste. It may be limited to just a back rub, or it may be a lingering, creative caressing of your mate's body, from head to toe. A little lotion or baby oil works well as a lubricant and contributes a pleasant scent. This is a beautiful way of loving your mate with your fingers, relishing each caress. And be sure you get a massage, too.

A warm bath or shower does much to relax and renew. Sharing this experience can be a very satisfying way of touching each other with love. Washing or even scrubbing your mate's body is somewhat like a massage. You can communicate your admiration for his or her body and your affection by the way you touch. Bathing your mate can be not only a rewarding way to end a long day but also a delightful way to prepare for lovemaking.

## Children

Just as we can give a recognition touch to a mate before arising, we can touch our children first thing in the morning as an affectionate greeting. We can give it when we awaken them or meet them going into the bathroom. Depending upon the age, sex, and personality of the child, the recognition touch could be a kiss, hug, caress, pat, tickle, playful poke, or arm lock. Once again, creativity and ingenuity are needed. Or it might be at breakfast when we offer our first tactual communication of the day. We can take a walk around the table, touching one member of the family lightly on the arm, the other gently on the shoulder, and another softly on the head or back of the neck. If you are using this approach for the first time, more may be accomplished by not making your efforts too obvious. This touching activity works well as a greeting and sign of recognition, especially if it is clarified with an expression like "Morning!" or "Sleep well?"

Grooming our children can be an occasion to express caring and reassurance. While we adjust their clothing, inspect fingernails, or check behind the ears, we must not fail to infuse the grooming gesture with regard and love. Similarly, we can cup the young one's chin in our hands and take a look at the teeth, or do a quick check of the hair to ferret out tangles and straighten crooked parts; these are good opportunities to show affection, particularly if we share our feelings at the time or respond to the child's emotions. The grooming gesture can be expanded to strokes of the head and face. When done properly, this touching is perhaps one of the most profound ways of expressing love nonverbally.

As we enter into these grooming activities with our children, we must remember that touching, to communicate effectively, must be expressed in sincerity and honesty. We must not falsify the original intent of our gestures. Initially, an inspection should be for the purpose of reviewing clothing and grooming, not just for touching. Once this is accomplished, we introduce our second intention—of communicating affection. If we do not make our first and second intentions clear, children will catch on very quickly and assume that our sole purpose is to touch them just to be touching. If they are noncuddlers or nontouchers, they may then resist our touches altogether. We must sincerely have a valid intention for the two types of touching: (1) instrumental touching, like the kind doctors and nurses use in medically serving patients; and (2) affective touching, to communicate emotions and feelings.

Children's morning departures offer a great chance to use touching to communicate well-wishing and encouragement. Children will be better able to face the day's challenges when they have been fortified with a big hug from their parents. We are reminded of this by the bumper stickers that say in big, bold letters: *HAVE YOU HUGGED YOUR KID TODAY?*

Some children demonstrate that they do not want to be hugged. They may pull away or react by saying: "Oh, Mom, I don't like to be hugged; that's for kids." If your child is this way, don't conclude that there is something wrong with him or her, or with you. It may be that the child is by nature a noncuddler and still exhibits the related characteristics. Or hugging may seem threatening because of the attitudes of peers; hugging such a child within sight of friends may subject him or her to ridicule. If you suspect that such is the case, limit your hugging to times and places when playmates are not present. If your child still resists hugging, try some other form of tactual contact, such as tickling, rough play, or an affectionate tug of the hair.

The evening meal lends itself to improvement of interpersonal and family relations through touch. If we affectionately touch the children as we greet them before dinner, we communicate our interest in becoming closer to them. A natural way of doing this is to come up behind them at the table and squeeze a shoulder or upper arm or tickle to the back of the neck. Generally, this meal moves at a slower pace than breakfast and allows more time to reflect and exchange ideas. During the leisure time of the meal, light pats to the upper arms and shoulders convey reassurance. To be effective, the recipient must not feel that the touches are an intrusion, such as "pounding" or "forced touching," but are natural gestures given and received in a caring way.

A mealtime touching activity in which family members extend and hold hands in a circle greatly enhances bonding into a closer unity. On a visit to Memphis, Tennessee, I saw several families do this. After all members had arrived at the table, they all joined hands as they were led in prayer. Joining hands says in a nonverbal way: "We are united in our recognition of one another as individuals and confirm that the individual is a vital link in this family."

Contacts between parents and children in later evening hours are optimal, especially in getting ready for bed. The evening bath, the washing and drying of little faces and bodies, is an excellent occasion to express tenderness and loving care. Tucking children in bed is also an opportunity to communicate assurance and security through loving touches and a goodnight kiss. Children who have experienced those loving touches associated with bedtime tend to sleep with greater ease and comfort and have a much greater chance of waking with a cheery and hope-filled attitude.

## Teenage Children

Teenage years are a very sensitive time for touching exchanges because of the profound significance of sexual development and striving for independence that the young person is experiencing. During this difficult transition period, young people need recognition, reassurance, and love but not in any form that smacks of childishness. For this reason, we should use adult modes of touching, such as handshakes, pats on the back, and shoulder hugs, with our teenage children. It might also be well to link a verbal compliment with the more affectionate touches, giving recognition to the maturing that is taking place. Teenage boys who are developing muscles and/or growing tall by leaps and bounds enjoy a touch to the upper arm muscle or shoulder, coupled with a comment about their amazing new physique or height. Fathers can also interact physically with their teenage sons through sports. A teenage girl might enjoy an arm around the waist or a squeeze around the shoulders from either parent, with a comment about what an attractive young woman she is becoming.

## Older Persons

Older persons, whether they be parents, other relatives, friends, or just acquaintances, have a great need for tactual communication. Unfortunately, many people tend to avoid touching older people. Many older persons have lost some of their verbal ability; yet they can still communicate through touch. Research has shown that the nonverbal communication of childhood can once again become the major avenue of communication (Preston 1973). Many older people have lost people close to them through death; for this reason, they have an acute need for love, affection, and companionship. A warm handshake, hug, or kiss on the cheek may communicate caring in a way that is more meaningful than we can imagine. Studies of persons in geriatric institutions show not only their hunger for affection but also the great value they place on the smallest gesture, the simplest touch (Burnside 1973). A study of geriatric patients' responses to different types of touch showed that the least agreeable gesture among seven was placing the arm around the shoulders; the most preferred gesture was a touch to the arm (DeWever 1977). Perhaps the people in the study felt that an arm around their shoulders impled inadequacy or dependency in some way and was perceived as demeaning. These studies seem to tell us that we should offer many loving touches to older relatives and friends, particularly those who have lost any part of the speech faculty. We must be careful not to communicate pity or overprotectiveness, but rather sincere love and companionship.

For new acquaintances, the handshake is generally the best way to communicate friendship and avoid causing discomfort. The bonding of the friendship can be enhanced by not only shaking hands but also cupping the free hand over the handshake. There is no rule for when to introduce this added gesture of warmth other than to be sensitive to the individual.

A less common variation of the standard handshake might be interesting to try in a social situation. In this gesture, instead of extending the right hand, extend the opened left hand, allowing the other person to clasp it with the right hand. The touch resembles jointly holding hands instead of shaking hands, subtly communicating "being with" the other person. The standard handshake has become so perfunctory in most social and personal exchanges that it has diluted the purpose of shaking hands. This variation gives us a great opportunity to apply our full attention to the meaning of the exchange. By this handshake modification, we can communicate the special meaning "I am with you" to a new acquaintance. This type of handshake can also be used as a parting gesture.

## Colleagues

Greeting our associates upon arrival at work is an occasion to extend recognition and fellowship in touching gestures. This is aptly accomplished in the aerospace industry, for example. One man approaches another, giving him a light tap with a closed fist to his upper arm. A gesture of this nature is usually done in a jocular way, as if to feign boxing. From the viewpoint of the men as well as observers, these contacts are not considered "sissified" and do not threaten their masculinity. Rather, they effectively communicate recognition and fellowship.

Whereas men frequently use such rough-play types of greetings, women are often not so inclined. A woman can greet a male colleague by coming up behind and grabbing hold of his shoulder. Another gesture a woman can use with a colleague of either sex is a gentle grab of the elbow from behind or beside the person or a tap on the lower arm while facing the person. These gestures can also be used by men in greeting male or female colleagues. Touches to the arms and shoulders, especially brief taps, are most neutral in terms of sexual implications and can be used quite freely without much chance of misinterpretation. Ordinarily, though, such gestures are not initiated by an inferior to a superior. In the case of a superior, it is normally more appropriate to offer a simple handshake; rank is not a deterrent to this exchange.

Some colleagues have adopted the African handshake, which is quite popular, particularly in the Black culture of the United States. One version is completed by the slapping of two people's flat palms together. In another version, hands are first clasped in a regular handshake, followed by an interlocked cupping of the fingers of each participant; this movement is either preceded or followed by a spinning of thumbs. Such an elaborate greeting requires considerable coordination; each person has to move his or her hand, fingers, and thumb within the same time frame for the shake to be effective. Such a gesture can be very rewarding, since it communicates not only a greeting but also fellowship and togetherness.

Effective touching enhances meetings involving fellow employees. If people are milling around for a few minutes before a meeting, we can communicate welcome and recognition in a handshake or some other gesture as already described. Sometimes our peers hesitate to do this. They may feel it's "too political" or ludicrous to shake hands with colleagues they see every day. But why get locked into this negative thinking? It is so easy to take a positive perspective and verbalize the message we wish to communicate clearly. It's simple enough. Just say, "I wanted to come over and say 'hello' while I had a chance."

Luncheon engagements lend themselves to an abundance of touch communication. Sitting close together around a table lets us emphasize our interest in others. Periodically placing the hands on top of their arms, patting lightly, assures them of our interest in their discussion. This is not to suggest that we touch indiscriminately. The suggestion is to touch with sincerity, and not with ulterior motives but with unobtrusive, caring gestures.

If we are not already in the habit, it is a good idea to incorporate patting the back or shoulders into our relationships with colleagues. Technological advancement and mass production have taken away much of the individual's sense of pride in accomplishment and creativity. Little reward or sincere recognition is given to individuals, as their unique efforts are almost unidentifiable. So when friends or associates accomplish a difficult and unique task, it's a good idea to give them that literal pat on the back to show our recognition and appreciation of their achievement.

## Close Friends

Communication through touch is a rewarding aspect of close friendship. There is no limit to the variety of ways we can use touch to enrich these relationships. When we go beyond the types of touching that are characteristic with acquaintances and colleagues, many of us have one concern: we need clarity as to the presence or absence of sexual implications. In same-sex friendships, men seem more threatened by the fear of homosexuality than women; thus, men are more restrained in their use of touch with close friends of the same sex. Whether male or female, though, before incorporating new touching interactions with a close friend or roommate, we should talk it over with the friend. In this way, we can clarify our intentions, avoid misinterpretation, and seek to grow together. If we are unable to discuss such a matter with the friend, perhaps we should not introduce such a touching exchange into the relationship.

With opposite-sex friends, similar verbal communication is necessary to clarify whether or not new touching exchanges are intended to express sexual interest. There are some ways of expressing companionship or affection that do not necessarily imply that the relationship is a sexual one. One such behavior is linking arms or joining hands. Such signs of fellowship are most acceptable when dancing or singing in a group or as a symbol of unity in a ceremony. In certain situations in our culture, a pair of female friends may link arms as they stroll along, perhaps conversing in a park or window-shopping. Linking arms is a much more common expression of companionship among opposite-sex friends; it can be a very enjoyable way of being together.

Kissing on the cheek is a common expression of affection among opposite-sex friends and, in certain circles, among female friends. Another variation is the cheek-to-cheek kiss used among women and opposite-sex friends in French cultures to express a greeting or congratulations. One person presses part of the cheek and lips against the cheek of the other person while placing both forearms beneath those of the other person; the second person responds by taking hold of the other's arms and perhaps lightly pecking him or her on the cheek. Some female friends find it natural to greet or take leave of each other with a peck on the cheek or pressing their cheeks together, coupled with a partial or full embrace.

A simple embrace used in Mexico and in many Spanish-speaking countries of Central and South America has been adopted by many North Americans. It is referred to as *el abrazo*. The participants embrace and simultaneously pat each other on the back. The embrace, extended to family members and close friends in opposite-sex and same-sex pairs, usually accompanies greetings and farewells. When opposite-sex pairs embrace, contact consists of touching the shoulders, with little or no breast or chest contact, thus reducing the potential for a sexual interpretation. Uniquely, this embrace is acceptable among male friends. *El abrazo* could very easily be introduced among close friends and family members if we tell them about its friendship-bonding effects in Spanish-speaking cultures. We might tell them that we wish to incorporate the embrace into our greetings and departures. Then, we could use it as a cordial and friendly recognition. After introducing the embrace and continuing this behavior for a while, we may find our friends willing to share their sentiments about the experience. Chances are that their responses will be very positive, because they will have experienced an affinity difficult to communicate through words alone.

# PART TWO

# TOUCHING LITERATURE

Part II contains condensations of some formal research in the field as well as summaries of popular articles on touching. These have been grouped into five thematic categories:

- Physiological Foundations and Perceptual Applications of Touch. This research discusses the sensory aspects of touch (Chapter 11).

- Touch in the Early Years. These studies present touch in the developmental stages from infancy through early adolescence (Chapter 12).

- Touch in the Sexual Encounter: Male/Female Orientations. The articles in this section address the attitudes of men and women toward touch and the interplay between touch and sexual relating (Chapter 13).

- Self-Realization and Human Interaction through Touch. This research describes the importance of touch in the attainment of self-awareness and in interpersonal communication (Chapter 14).

- The Place of Touch in Physical and Emotional Health. This section deals with the significance of the use of touch in medicine and psychotherapy (Chapter 15).

# chapter eleven

# Physiological Foundations and Perceptual Applications of Touch

PAUL BUISSERET
*"The Six Senses"*

Discussing our bodies' peripheral sensations, Buisseret notes that the sensation of touch seems to depend upon several receptor organs. The distribution or concentration of these receptors varies according to the tissues in which they are located.

He describes three types of touch receptors:

1. *Capsular receptors.* These receptors "respond to deformation of their structure by firing off impulses along the sensory nerves arising from them, and thus are activated by touch, pressure, vibration, etc."

2. *Tactile corpuscles of Meissner.* One of the most abundant of the mechanoreceptors, these corpuscles predominate in the skin of the hand, the foot, the front of the forearm, the lips, the

From *Nursing Mirror Supplement,* January 26, 1978, pp. iii-iv.

eyelids, the conjunctivae (the mucous membranes of the eyes), and the tip of the tongue. These corpuscles are the receptors where the sense of touch is most acute.

3. *Lamellated corpuscles of Pacini.* These corpuscles, which are primarily concerned with touch, are found in the skin on the bottom of the foot, the fingers and toes, the genital organs, the arm, the neck, and the nipples. The corpuscles are also found in the sensitive area surrounding the bones.

"Two-point discrimination," says Buisseret, is a factor in our sense of touch (see chart that follows). A sharp, two-pointed compass, its points placed at varying distances over our skin, allows us to feel the two distinct points at the same time. As the two points are gradually moved together, they reach a position where we feel them as one single touch. "The more touch receptors there are in the skin to which the points are applied, the closer together they need to be before they feel just like a single point." The tip of the tongue and the pads of the fingertips appear to have the highest number of receptors, as the separation of the points on the compass is reduced to 1 mm on the tongue and 2 mm on the pads of the fingertips before we perceive them as one touch. The middle of the back appears to have a much smaller dispersion of receptors, as the two points on the compass are felt as one touch when the points are separated by 67 mm.

### Two-Point Discrimination Chart

| *Skin Area* | *Separation of Points in Millimeters* |
| --- | --- |
| Tip of Tongue | 1 |
| Pad of Fingertips | 2 |
| Palm of Hand | 11 |
| Back of Hand | 32 |
| Back of Neck | 54 |
| Middle of Back | 67 |

Thus the pads of the fingertips are more highly sensitive to touch than the skin on the back of the hand.

A person may vary from day to day or from one time of day to another in the two-point discrimination test. We are less discriminating late in the evening than in the morning. We are also less discriminating after a meal than when we are hungry. "Women are more discriminating just before a menstrual period than immediately afterwards."

The author also describes the characteristics and location of temperature receptors and pain receptors. There is a specific type of receptor (bulbous corpuscles of Krause) that is sensitive to a decrease in temperature. Another type of receptor (Golgi–Mazzoni), located primarily in the external genitals and the inside of the eyelid, is sensitive to increases in temperature. Buisseret explains that there are fewer receptors sensitive to temperature in the mouth than on the finger. This explains why we can drink a cup of tea without feeling discomfort "at a temperature which would be painful to the dipped finger. . . ."

"Pain may be perceived as having a pricking, burning, or itching quality depending upon how strongly the free nerve endings are stimulated." Pressure to produce pain may be measured in grams per square millimeter.

Distribution of pain receptors, he says, is quite different from distribution of touch receptors, as shown in the following chart.

| Tissue | *Pressure in grams per square millimeter* |
|---|---|
| Cornea | 0.2 |
| Conjunctiva | 2.0 |
| Abdominal skin | 15.00 |
| Back of hand | 100.00 |
| Sole of foot | 200.00 |
| Fingertip | 300.00 |

Considerably more pressure is required to evoke a pain on the fingertip than would be required to evoke a pain in the cornea.

PHILLIP W. DAVIDSON AND TERESA T. WHITSON
*"Haptic Equivalence Matching of Curvature by Blind and Sighted Humans"*

In the perception of curvatures, blind subjects are generally more accurate than blindfolded sighted subjects. This difference in sense perception between blind and sighted persons becomes more pronounced as the tasks become more difficult. It was found that the scanning strategy of the blind, which included gripping and using three or four fingers simultaneously, could be taught to the sighted. Using this strategy, sighted subjects improved their perception.

JAMES J. GIBSON
*"Observations on Active Touch"*

In his article, Gibson defines "active touch" as that activity normally called "touching," and he distinguishes "passive touch" as the act of being touched. He says that active touch denotes exploration rather than reception; it does not change the environment but creates a change in the sense perception of the environment.

Active touch may be likened to the movements of the eyes, a type of tactile scanning similar to visual scanning; hence, it is used by the blind to gain information about their world. The blind's use of touch contributes to their unique sixth sense, which is referred to as *haptics.*

In 1950, the researcher Revesz, who coined the term *haptics,* suggested that the hand is a type of sense organ, different from the skin on the hand. It is capable of tracing lines and shapes and other specific components of objects. The hand, in exploratory movements, singles out one subject and enhances the perception of it by repeated and intensified touching.

Gibson explains that active touching activates sense receptors in tendons and joints, in addition to receptors in the skin. Thus active touch may be distinguished from passive touch, which involves sense receptors only in the skin and underlying tissue. The factor of location of the fingers, hand, arm, body, and head in relation to the object and to gravity also has a bearing on the complete sensation.

Gibson emphasized that touch is completely separate from the senses of taste, smell, hearing, and seeing. It is realized through even the slightest deformation of the skin but can diminish if the skin is left motionless. Sense receptors, so potentially active, simply stop firing when left in disuse.

He found a lack of research data on the mechanical happenings associated with touching the skin surfaces. Most studies have used solid substances to determine impact on the skin, and little effort has been given to the study of the impact of air puffs or drops of water on the skin.

Gibson lists three types of mechanical events used to stimulate the skin: brief events of pushing, slapping, patting, tapping, placing pressure, and pricking; prolonged events without displacement—including acts of stretching, kneading, pinching, and vibrating; prolonged events with displacement—acts such as rubbing, scraping, scratching, sliding, rolling, and brushing. It is to be noted that these three events, with their relevant activities, vary in the amount of friction, stretching, and vertical depression of the skin surfaces. All the events involve the surface of an object touching or coming into contact with the skin.

After considering the three types of events that are stimulating to the skin, the author goes on to note two of the most fundamental aspects of touching: (1) our constant contact with the earth gives us a reassuring sense of support; the earth is our stable referent; and (2) the sensations and feelings received from passive and active touching are substantially different from each other. In the case of passive touching, two separate pressures are felt when two objects are applied to the skin. With active touching, on the other hand, there is a unity of touch. Two or more separate pressures can occur from the fingers, but the impressions are perceived as one object. With this type of touching, a feeling of the stability of the object exists, and we can feel its rigidity or lack of rigidity, as we receive a sensation of softness or elasticity. Active touching of the corners or edges of an object can also bring us an acute sense of awareness of the object.

Gibson points out that passive touch does yield a perception of something moving when a stimulus is drawn over it. He also notes that when "outlined" forms—such as the rim of a cup—and solid forms—such as a flat-bottom surface of a cup—are pressed into the skin, the outlined forms are more easily discernible.

The author's conclusions are substantiated by K. S. Lashley's finding that objects that are difficult to perceive through passive touch can readily be perceived through active touch. Gibson extends this notion, adding that accurate identification is more reliable through active touch (95 percent) than through passive touch (49 percent).

He describes three correlations between active touch and vision:

1. Surfaces that are solid can be determined by touch and sight. There are some surfaces, like smoke, that are only visible and not tangible. Another may be tangible (like plate glass) and not visible. Others that vary between touch and vision are color, which is intangible, and temperature, which is invisible.

2. Vision can give only the perception of the front surfaces of objects, whereas touch can perceive both fronts and backs of surfaces simultaneously.

3. Curvatures and edges of corners may be perceived equally by sight and touch. Any differences in perception by touch can be confirmed by sight.

**162**

Gibson concludes: "In general, experimenters have not realized that to apply a stimulus to an observer is not the same as for an observer to obtain the stimulus."

DAVID L. LANDRIGAN AND G. ALFRED FORSYTH
*"Regulation and Production of Movement Effects in Exploration-Recognition Performance"*

Landrigan and Forsyth's study sought to determine what it is about active touch that makes it a more accurate means of perception than passive touch. They compared two aspects of active touch: production-of-movement and regulation-of-movement. Production-of-movement refers to the physical initiation of the touching activity. Regulation-of-movement refers to the control and direction of the course of the scanning. They found that the self-regulated aspect of the active touching movement was more significant for accurate perception than the self-production of the movement. Their study supports and extends the work of Gibson, who emphasized the primacy of active touching as opposed to passive touching for perception.

PAT MUELLER
*"Doing It the Hard Way"*

Blindfolded students in Mueller's pottery ceramics class found that it was possible to control the clay on a potter's wheel by using the sense of touch. Some of the finished products were as good as those produced by students without blindfolds. Actually, a few students produced better products without seeing. Mueller

Landrigan and Forsyth from *Journal of Experimental Psychology*, 103 (1974), 1124-1130. Copyright 1974 by the American Psychological Association. Reprinted by permission.

Mueller from *School Arts*, January 1975 pp. 41-42.

**163**

suggests that exclusively using the sense of touch aids in establishing greater control of clay manipulation. Students also acquired, according to Mueller, a greater appreciation for the "lesser" sensory mechanism of touch, which invariably goes unheeded because of the predominance of the senses of sight and hearing.

# chapter twelve

# Touch in the Early Years

SOL ADLER
*The Non-Verbal Child*

Adler advises that a sequence of events must occur in order for communicative behavior to develop. He aptly states: "Sensitivity becomes sensation when one is aware of the stimulus and responds to it (covertly or overtly). The child's first responses are undifferentiated mass movements that are innate and reflexive. As growth and maturation occur, the child develops increasing ability to differentially respond to stimulation; that is, the child learns to recognize or perceive certain sensations and to make appropriate adjustments to them."

Infants have an innate ability to "perceive" relationships in the physical world; however, they must also "learn" relationships. Infants learn through testing their senses. Most of the early learning is through trial and error or by stimulus–response. The

From Sol Adler, *The Non-Verbal Child*, 1964. Courtesy of Charles C Thomas, Publisher, Springfield, Illinois.

infant also learns to recognize and discriminate objects by touching them. The infant's first learned concepts are "concrete" because they refer to his or her immediate (tactile) world. The infant learns a sense of symbolization, an "inner language." Symbols refer to "something" and are encoded. Infants use tactile symbols for receptive language until about the ninth month, when they develop verbal receptive language. Active tactile expression is replaced by verbal expressive language when the child utters the first words, some time around the first year of life.

Adler points out that recognizing and discriminating objects by touch is a significant sensory element for the learning child. It is possible to identify tactile dysfunction via simple tests. Passive tactile dysfunction may be determined by touching the child while his or her eyes are closed and asking for an indication of the part of the body being touched. Tests for active tactile dysfunction should include having the child "feel" specific objects without simultaneously seeing them and later identify the objects felt from a group of objects. The child should feel objects with each hand first and then with both hands, so that the examiner may discover unilateral or bilateral tactile variation. Adler suggests that examiners diagnose tactile symbolization impairment by placing different objects in the child's hand and asking how they are used—for example, a pencil, for writing; a key, for opening a door.

LAWRENCE GALTON
*"For Mother and Child—Closer Encounters"*

Opportunities for bonding of parents with newborn infants are increasing. Galton reports on a young mother in a Chicago hospital. Directly after the delivery, her baby was transferred to the care of the father, who cut the umbilical cord and proceeded

From *Parade*, October 1, 1978, pp. 5-8.

to bathe the child. Both parents were joyous at being able to spend these first hours with their baby in the homelike birthing room instead of separating themselves from the child (the mother going to the recovery room, the father returning home, and the child staying in a nursery).

Galton reports that immediate bonding of mothers with their newborn babies offers important benefits. He cites the early twentieth-century findings of Dr. Pierre C. Budin, which suggest that the separation of mothers from their newborn infants results in a loss of the natural maternal bond. Researchers studying mother–infant bonding have continued to investigate and question the psychological effects of interrupting the interaction of the newborn and parent.

Galton emphasizes the importance of the first few minutes and hours of a child's life. Current research shows that an infant must have close contact with the mother during the first few hours of life. This contact facilitates a beautiful linking between mother and child and full development of the child's potential in later years.

Doctors have reported many benefits of early bonding.

At 1, 3, 6, 9, and 12 months, the bonded babies gained more weight and had fewer infections. . . .

At two years after birth, the long-contact mothers spoke to their children with a greater number of words and questions and with fewer commands than did the other mothers —which seemed to have implications for intellectual development.

And at five years, the long-contact children had higher IQ's and superior scores on language tests.

There is some evidence that bonding between the infant and the father is similarly favorable.

DOROTHY GRAVES
*"Right from the Start"*

The first three years of a child's life are most important, claims Dorothy Graves. "What happens or fails to happen during that time determines in large measure what the child becomes or fails to become."

She states: "No list or chart can possibly convey the life-sustaining force of Mother's tenderness, Father's smile, their fondling of the child. . . . Right from the start, the child experiences through the sense of touch the feeling of being loved and wanted. . . . ." In contrast, she cites a recent study showing that parents, in fact, give fewer signs of affection to their children than one would think.

The study showed that upper-class mothers demonstrated the most frequent spontaneous touching, whereas the working-class mothers gave children the second most frequent touching, and the middle-class mothers gave the least. Children just beginning to walk received the most contact.

Frequency of touch was also broken down according to the children's placement in the family. The group that received the most frequent affectionate touches were older children in upper-class families; those receiving the least were the youngest children in working-class families.

Graves recommends that we make time to provide the loving touches our children need in order to feel safe and secure. We should rock, stroke, and cuddle our children generously. "Out of our fondling the child and giving him a sense of being loved and cared for, he himself develops a capacity for loving." Although this fondling provides the child with the security he or she needs, it cannot be overdone to the point of inculcating unwholesome dependence.

From *The PTA Magazine*, 63 (May 1969), 22-24.

MARK L. KNAPP
*"The Effects of Touching Behavior on Human Communication"*

Knapp gives an overview of many significant studies on human touching. In discussing touching as it relates to human development, Knapp says that our sense of touch may be the first sense in our life experience; it is the first means of knowing what living is going to be like. As babies newly arrived in the world, we experience hands touching us. Hands feed, bathe, rock, and comfort us. Progressively, in childhood, touch is accompanied by words, and we formulate an association with the two means of communication. We later reach a point in our childhood development when words begin to replace touch as a means of communication. When this occurs, we replace the intimacy and closeness of touching with a more distant communication through words. There is also some evidence that verbal symbols not validated through touching in the course of development are less clear and less effective symbols for communication in later years. For example, those of us who have never touched snow have a less clear concept of the word *snow* than those of us who have walked and played in it. It seems that we need to make the meanings of the words we use concrete through touch.

At what point do babies receive more touching? Knapp reports on some conflicting findings from various researchers regarding the age at which babies receive more touch stimulation and whether boys and girls receive more touching during infancy.

Knapp, however, finds more consensus among researchers on the pattern of touching of the school-age child. From kindergarten through the sixth grade, touching activity is on a steady decline. Yet touching activity during this period is still greater than that of adults. Youngsters in junior high schools exhibit about half the touching activity of youth in primary grades. Touching activities among youth in the primary grades are more frequently initiated with hands. Shoulder-to-shoulder and elbow-to-elbow contacts replace the hand-initiated contact for junior-high students. Knapp reports an "inactive" period in touching after childhood. The inactive period is replaced by more interest in touching in adolescence, when tactile experience with the opposite sex becomes more attractive.

Early touching experiences appear to be highly significant to later developmental activities. Infants receiving infrequent touching tend to walk later. Retardation in speech and reading have been correlated to early deprivation of touching. The evidence points to the idea that infant and childhood tactile satisfaction is a basic requirement for healthy development.


H. R. SCHAFFER AND PEGGY E. EMERSON
*"Patterns of Response to Physical Contact in Early Human Development'*

Schaffer and Emerson underscore the importance to the young of physical contact. They refer to other writers who identified rocking, stroking, cuddling, and holding as activities essential for the psychological growth of children. Infants who do not have close body contact with their mothers are subject to touch deprivation, a potential hindrance in later development.

Schaffer and Emerson conducted a study of infants' reactions to physical contact. This study led them to a striking finding: "that not all infants eagerly seek physical contact . . . indeed that a considerable proportion of the subjects actively resisted and protested. . . ."

Thirty-seven infants a few weeks old became the subjects of

From *Journal of Child Psychology and Psychiatry*, 5, (1964), 1-13.

the study. Their mothers were interviewed once every four weeks through the infants' first twelve months; the mothers were interviewed once more when the child was eighteen months old. The findings reported in this article, however, were drawn from the data obtained in the two interviews at the end of the 12-month and 18-month periods only.

In the interviews, the mothers were asked to report on the following:

a) "the infant's behavior in a number of commonly occurring contact situations, such as being cuddled, carried, held on lap, stroked, kissed, fed on knee, and swung or bounced;

b) "the consistency of these reactions with age, person offering the contact, and the infant's internal condition (i.e., the effect of pain, illness, fatigue or fear);

c) "evidence for contact-seeking in relation to inanimate objects or the self;

d) "the mother's behavior in contact situations and her reactions to any contact avoidance on the infant's part."

Nineteen of the thirty seven infants (approximately 50 percent) accepted, enjoyed, and actively sought physical contact; these were categorized as the "cuddlers." Nine of the infants (approximately 25 percent) were found to be "noncuddlers"; they consistently resisted cuddling, even when tired, frightened, in pain, or ill. The remaining nine infants were somewhat in the middle; they accepted limited cuddling when tired and ill. The generalizations drawn from the study were obtained by comparing the cuddler group with the noncuddler group.

In contrast to the cuddlers' behavior, the noncuddlers would become restless, struggle, and turn their faces away when being cuddled. They even resisted merely being held on the knee. In times of distress, the only consolation they would respond to positively was some form of distraction, such as being given a biscuit or a bottle or being walked or diverted through play.

With respect to feeding, there was no difference in the cuddlers' and noncuddlers' responses to being held while being given a bottle during the first six months. After six months, only two of the noncuddlers resisted being fed on their mothers' laps.

Noncuddlers did not resist all forms of skin contact. They were receptive to kisses and affectionate stroking as long as it did not involve being picked up. They actually enjoyed activity involving contact but not restraint, such as tickling, swinging, and romping. It seems that restriction of movement, not contact, is being avoided.

Schaffer and Emerson attempted to determine whether environmental or congenital factors were the root cause of cuddler behavior. With respect to an environmental cause, there was no correlation between a mother's preference for touching her child and the child's being identified as a cuddler or noncuddler. As a matter of fact, cuddler infants with nontouching mothers sought contact with other family members. Intrinsic characteristics of general restlessness, a tendency to sleep less, and earlier motor development (sitting up, standing, crawling, and so on) of noncuddlers points to the possibility that there is a congenital predisposition for their behavior. These findings, coupled with the fact that noncuddlers showed no signs of seeking substitutes for cuddling in soft toys, favorite blankets, or self-touching, lead to the conclusion that the origin of cuddler behavior is not environmental or social, but rather congenital.

Schaffer and Emerson conclude as follows:

1. Infant cuddlers, in particular, require affectionate, close contact to assure appropriate developmental progress.
2. Noncuddlers fulfill their touching needs through walking around and rough play.
3. If parents find that their infant does not respond to hugging and cuddling, they should seek other less restraining ways to interact physically with him or her.

PAUL WEISBERG
*"Developmental Differences in Children's Preferences for
High- and Low-arousing Forms of Contact Stimulation"*

Weisberg hypothesized that children from three to seven
years old would exhibit a developmental transition from prefer-
ring cuddling (low-arousing stimulation) to tickling (high-
arousing stimulation) from an adult. He also felt that the sex of
the adult providing the stimulation would relate to the sex of the
child, with the preference for contact with an adult of the same
sex increasing with the age of the child. He attributed sex-role
stereotypes to adult men and women, viewing tickling stimulation
as more characteristic of men and cuddling as more characteristic
of women.

In keeping with these assumptions, Weisberg set up an experiment involving eighty boys and eighty girls, in four age
groups between three and seven, selected from nursery schools
and a first-grade class. The children were taken to a room in the
school setting where a male adult and a female adult awaited
them. The children were drawn into play by the adults and given
tickling or cuddling stimulation, each treatment being given to
each child three times. There were ten adult contact agents, and
each served equally as cuddler and tickler among the four age
groups of children. At a later time, the children were given the opportunity to choose between the two adults.

The children showed a significant preference for tickling
with increasing age, in support of Weisberg's hypothesis. The
youngest girls preferred a female adult, whether she offered cuddling or tickling stimulation. Weisberg recommended further experimentation that would separate the factor of sex from the type
of stimulation.

From *Child Development*, 46 (1975), 975-979.

RAYMOND K. YANG AND THOMAS C. DOUTHITT
*"Newborn Responses to Threshold Tactile Stimulation"*

Yang and Douthitt report on their clinical study of the heart-rate response of babies to "air-puff" tactile stimulation. Newborn babies were given air-puff tactile stimulation with increasing intensity until a motor response (threshold) was obtained. At the prethreshold level, no heart-rate changes were observed. The average threshold required .085 pounds per square inch, which was substantially below the pressure needed to cause an indentation of the skin. The body movement response to threshold-level stimulation was accompanied by an increase in heart rate. Increases in heart rate at threshold levels for subjects averaged twenty beats per minute, peaking between nine and twelve seconds after stimulation. All babies demonstrated increased heart rates at the threshold, with no variation found resulting from sex differences or threshold level.

In this study, Yang and Douthitt attempted to discover in babies a level of touching stimulation that would produce nondefensive orienting (decelerated) responses. They found that individual response curves to the threshold-level stimulus showed that each subject reacted with an increased heart rate, and no subject's response reflected a decelerated response. Although no subjects demonstrated the nondefensive orienting response as hoped, their average increase in heart rate of twenty beats per minute was only about half the average heart-rate change elicited from newborns in other studies, where a more intense stimulus was given. Yang and Douthitt find this lesser change in heartbeat a provocative result.

From *Child Development*, 45 (1974), 237-242. Copyright 1974 by The Society for Research in Child Development Inc.

# chapter thirteen

# Touch in the Sexual Encounter: Male/Female Orientations

JUDITH DANCOFF
*"Beyond Sex: Can Women and Men Be Just Friends?"*

The trap of sexual conditioning frequently proves too tenacious for fostering friendly intentions between most men and women, writes Judith Dancoff. Though well matched and in need of companions, men and women frequently pass up chances for friendship.

Ms. Dancoff illustrates her point with an example from her own personal life. From their first meeting, all she and her new acquaintance really wanted was to be friends. Acting on the values of the sexual revolution of the sixties, with all its expected patterns of behavior, they locked themselves into "an absurdist comedy." Without the appropriate sexual enthusiasm for each

From *Mademoiselle*, 81 (December 1975), 22, 80, 81. Copyright © 1975 by The Conde Nast Publications, Inc.

other, they went through the motions of a sexual encounter, only later to discover that they were destined not to be lovers but genuine friends. The writer concludes: "Friendships with others require a willingness to dispense with all the familiar roles and stereotypes ... and to see instead the actual person." It seems, she complains, that asking for a night of companionship has become more difficult than asking for a night of sex. She advises us, though, to give it a try. Many very rewarding friendships may be discovered in this way.


KAREN DURBIN
*"Beyond Sex: The Need to Touch"*

Durbin describes two personal experiences, both pertinent to touching. She and a male friend, having spent the day together in a spirit of trust and affection, observed that they "had been unconsciously careful not to touch each other." Finally her friend remarked that he was not afraid to touch if she was not, and the conversation continued with him shifting his feet to rest comfortably against her legs.

In another incident, feeling "a slight stab of loneliness" at an otherwise very happy party, Durbin was approached by a flamboyantly energetic old friend who engaged her in conversation while touching her "often in an exuberant, friendly way." She found his touching "gently erotic and very comforting." Inducing her to touch him back and making her feel "attractive and wanted," his touching took away her feeling of loneliness.

Reflecting on Americans' sadly restricted touching behavior, Durbin observes that we have learned "the lesson of an essentially Puritan culture (where everything has its purpose), that touching is purposefully, specifically sexual."

From *Mademoiselle*, 81 (December 1975), 78-79. Copyright © 1975 by The Conde Nast Publications, Inc.

Reflecting on her own childhood experience, Durbin comments that a child's world is full of tactile sensations. Children relate to things and people through touch. Somehow we eliminate this behavior from our adult lives. Durbin finds it paradoxical that our culture puts so much emphasis on sex; yet we Americans are not sensuous people. Her recommendation is that we recall our sensuous childhood ways and reinstate them in our adult lives.

MARC H. HOLLENDER, LESTER LUBORSKY, AND THOMAS J. SCARAMELLA
*"Body Contact and Sexual Enticement"*

Do women *use* sex for the purpose of being held and cuddled? The authors consider this question in their article, drawing on their own case studies and on evidence from other researchers.

Being cuddled and held tends to give one a feeling of security and to reduce anxiety, they point out, but the intensity of this need to be touched varies from one person to another, and it changes within individuals at various times. They found that among women, the intensity of this need can range from addiction, through mild desire, to indifference, and even to total repugnance at the thought of being touched.

The authors learned that needs for touching parallel oral needs in that each becomes more intensified during periods of anxiety. However, oral needs are easily satisfied with objects like cigars, cigarettes, food, and alcohol. Body-touching needs, in contrast, can rarely be satisfied without the contact of another person.

The authors conducted a study of thirty female psychiatric patients suffering from severe disorders. The women who scored high on a questionnaire measuring their desire to be held used sex in exchange for cuddling, report the authors, whereas the women

From *Archives of General Psychiatry*, 20 (February 1969), 188-191.

with a low investment in being held did not use sex as a motivation for touching. Other researchers confirm the preceding findings, reporting that many women feel that sexual activity is a price that has to be paid in order for them to be held or cuddled.

Other research, on severely disturbed patients seems to indicate that such persons use sex as a means to achieve human contact rather than to experience physical pleasure. In one case study, it was found that a chronic wrist cutter could escape the compulsion to cut her wrists by finding a male sex partner who would hold her. In another case, it was found that a woman with a strong desire for physical contact and body stimulation used prostitution and promiscuity to satisfy her needs.

The authors contend that the need for tender touching is prevalent not only among women under psychiatric treatment. They believe that many women invite their husbands into coitus or engage in promiscuous activity because they need to be held and cuddled. They explain this phenomenon by saying that the desire by mature adults to be held and cuddled in a parental manner is perceived as a taboo in our culture. Women thus conceal the desire or convert it to the desire for coitus, which is perceived as a more acceptable adult activity.

MARC H. HOLLENDER
*"The Need or Wish to Be Held"*

"The woman with a strong craving to be held often barters sex, giving the man what he desires (coitus) for what she desires (cuddling)." But women must sometimes suppress their desire to be held if they do not want to play the trading game, as they know that physical contact generally triggers interest in sexual activity in their partners.

In this article, Hollender reports on data received in interviews with twenty-seven paid female volunteers and twenty-seven female patients hospitalized for acute psychiatric problems. He found no generalized differences between the two groups in relation to body contact experiences. He studied the reasons for and the degree of the women's need for cuddling, the impact of their need on marital relationships and promiscuity, and the substitutes that sometimes replaced the cuddling they craved.

Tactile stimulation serves an important sexual purpose for women, says Hollender, much like sight stimulation for men. Nevertheless, most women also associate touch with feelings of security, comfort, protection, love, contentment, and overcoming aloneness. One woman said: "When I am held, I am very happy, very content and I feel very safe, and I feel that there is nothing in the world that can go wrong because I am being held." Others reported a release of tension similar to the relief of sexual intercourse.

Not all women crave cuddling or trade it for sex. Some care little about it, and others even shun it. Hollender points out that the need may fluctuate within the individual, too—one interview revealing the woman's increased interest during times of anxiety or depression.

The author considers the reasons for many women's strong need for touch. He quotes one woman who attributed her craving to a lack of parental touching during childhood, and he also points to the natural closeness that all children have *inside* the womb and long to continue on the *outside*.

A woman's self-image and personal goals also seem to affect her need or at least the way she expresses it. The author notes that women who are comfortable with their femininity appear to feel freer to express their desire to be held. There also seems to be a correlation between striving for independence and the desire to be held. The more one seeks out independence, the less one will have the desire to be held, as the desire to be held is viewed as childlike and reflective of dependence.

Some women hesitate to allow their mates to hold them in public, as they feel such an action is considered a form of sexual

From *Archives of General Psychiatry*, 22 (May 1970), 445-453. Copyright 1970 American Medical Association.

encounter and insist upon restricting it to private quarters. Anger toward their husbands decreases the desire of women to be held. They tend to maintain a distance until they start a truce in which touching may facilitate the feeling of closeness again.

How do women make the request for body contact? They either ask in so many words, or they nonverbally request the contact by sitting next to their mates, reaching out an arm to them, sitting on their laps, or simply snuggling close. Pouting or crying also appears to be an indirect yet effective way for some to request being held. Another less popular way is to pick an argument which could be followed by tactual closeness when the couple makes up.

Hollender reveals several substitutes women find for being held. Some women turn to their children and hold them. Some show a preference for substitute body stimulation by rocking, masturbating, or holding inanimate objects. Many others use oral substitutes such as eating, smoking, drinking, or talking to a friend on the phone. Still others bundle up in warm clothes or blankets, because it gives them a feeling of being held.

The author explains that the need or wish to be held may contribute to marital problems and promiscuity, plus a high number of illegitimate births. It is also linked to several psychiatric disorders; yet in the hierarchy of human needs, it has been given little attention. Clearly, researchers must do more than concentrate on oral needs as they have in the past.

WILLIAM H. MASTERS AND VIRGINIA E. JOHNSON
*"Touching: How Intimacy Is Born"*

The act of touching *can be* its own goal, explain Masters and Johnson. It links human lives and brings about a feeling of oneness to separated individuals. How human beings have

See pages 230-240 of *The Pleasure Bond: A New Look at Sexuality and Commitment,* 1974 (Boston: Little, Brown and Company).

distorted and diluted this function is explored in Chapter 10 of *The Pleasure Bond.*

Parents tend to give their infants "the stroking, snuggling, and enfolding movements with which almost all living creatures seek the warmth and reassurance that . . . is virtually indistinguishable from life itself." As the child begins to grow up a little, parents typically withhold kisses, "except as a formality," and discourage any snuggling in their lap. The children, however, continue to need these affectionate touches, although they learn the "don't touch" lesson nonverbally conveyed by the parents.

The meaning of touch is further depreciated when youngsters start the sex-touch game of "boy wins, girl loses." Far from communicating love, touching becomes simply a signal of "sexual provocation . . . a specific means to accomplish sexually specific goals." Young partners, keenly aware of their expected roles, concern themselves with image and skill, not communication. While the girl remains basically passive, seeking to avoid responsibility, the boy aims for that "triumphant awareness of doing what is forbidden, of touching those parts of a girl's body that are private and concealed. . . ." Small wonder, then, that the young boy's touchings are "closer to groping or grabbing than caressing" and often produce resistance instead of a "turn-on."

The first fumblings between the boy and girl that do not produce a "turn-on" cause both to question either themselves or their partner. This may lead to a continuing search for someone who will play the game with them, a person whose touches bring pleasure, who has the right technique. Not uncommonly, troubled adults revert to this stage, seeking the perfect sex mate.

Even most successful adult sex games are lacking, as both partners tend to think of touching as an exclusive means to an exclusive end—intercourse. The stroking and snuggling experienced in infancy are depreciated; their messages of caring and needing are replaced with mechanistic concerns of position, penetration, and "having a climax." Once they have an ongoing agreement with a mate, some men actually tend to regard touching as "an unnecessary postponement of intercourse."

In the past decade, sex partners, well read in the mechanics of sex, have been self-instructed in contact with another body but have failed to learn how to touch another human being caressingly. Thus, the mechanistic touch game leading to intercourse has converted people to objects and touching activities to a "science of stimulation." The joy of silent, intimate communication and the potential feeling of oneness fall victim to the confused struggle of players in the sex-touch game.

Instead of using affectionate touches to inspire trust and signal loving commitment, players often destroy bonds of communication. Those whose only goal is intercourse "overwhelm [the partner] with feelings of helplessness and outrage, of loneliness, worthlessness, and despair. . . ." Masters and Johnson contend that to be pleasurably alive, human beings require touching's nourishment just as they need the vital stimulation of their other senses. To lose touch is to lose one dimension of their humanness and to miss the profound rewards that intimacy brings.

TUAN NGUYEN, RICHARD HESLIN, AND MICHELE L. NGUYEN
*"The Meanings of Touch: Sex Differences"*

In "The Meanings of Touch: Sex Differences," the authors discuss their findings on the relationship between responses to touch and diverse factors ranging from gender to modes of touch and location.

The male body is less sensitive to the pressure of touching than the female body, they report, and males tend to consider touching almost any part of their bodies as playful or friendly. Females, on the other hand, take their bodies more seriously. They do not consider the touching of their breasts or genital areas

From *Journal of Communication*, Summer 1975, pp. 92-103.

as playful. Women often have negative responses to sexual touchings when they are single but strong positive responses when they are married.

In addition to sex and marital status, surroundings and professional roles may influence responses to touch. Nurses who regularly touch their patients, for example, stimulate more verbal interaction than those who do not. Clearly, the combination of a potential interaction between sexes and the professional role is operating.

The authors also focus on skin sensitivity, location, and methods of touch. They contend that sex areas are not as sensitive to touch as was originally believed. In other words, sex is not the whole story when it comes to sensitivity; the sensory activities of our sex touchings are limited. The thumb, for example, with a smaller area of skin surface than the breast is represented by a larger area of the cortex.

Touching of larger skin surfaces, such as the back, suggests friendship, fellowship, and playfulness. Touching the hand, particularly, suggests a wide variety of responses ranging from friendship and pleasure to warmth and love.

The location of the touch influences its message, especially in the area of sexuality and friendliness; however, the modality of the touch (patting, stroking, squeezing, and accidental brushing) bears an overriding effect on its message. For example, whereas stroking tends to communicate "love touching" and "sex touching," patting tends to convey friendship and playfulness. Consider the difference between a warm knee caress and a friendly knee pat. In most cases, the "how" definitely dominates the "where."

The authors accent the diversity of types of communication through touch by pointing out that opposite-sex friends touch nonsexual areas more frequently than they do sexual areas. To understand all of the possibilities of communication through these diverse touchings, we must learn the meanings of different touching modes as they apply to different body areas.

RUTH WINTER
*"How People React to Your Touch"*

The meanings of and restrictions on touch are the focus of Ruth Winter's article. Although we have not identified and categorized each type of touch, explains the author, we know that touch is regulated by unwritten rules. Discussing recent research by Richard Heslin of Purdue University, she describes these rules and people's typical responses to touching.

Socially structured or polite touching occurs within the limits of implicit but precise rules that dictate the degree of and appropriate circumstances for touching. Touching for conveying friendship and warmth is not as formalized as social touching; still, depending on the degree and the setting, it tends to be misinterpreted as contact for sex or love.

A great deal of misunderstanding occurs about friendship touching, love touching, and sex touching, because they overlap and because they resemble one another. In the process, communication can deteriorate, and partners can miss valuable, supportive messages.

Theoretically, "friendship touching" provides the greatest appreciation of another person. The active partner is restricted, however, because of the possible misinterpretation of his or her gestures. Restrictions diminish when the partner is sufficiently sensitive to recognize distinctions between types of touching.

Obviously, there are clear-cut polarities in types and locations of touching; caressing the genitals creates greater sexual arousal than casually holding hands. Between these extremes lie many variations, with responses depending on such factors as the receiver's background, familiarity with the partner, marital status, and gender. Single males, for instance, differ from single females in their responses to touch on certain areas of their

From *Science Digest,* 79 (March 1976), 46-56.

bodies. Married male and female responses differ even more significantly.

It appears that passive sex touching is more pleasant to married women than single college women. The initiation of sex touching by wives tends to threaten husbands and create anxiety about their sexual performance ability and masculinity.

Heslin's research focuses on gender and marital status, but concentrates even more on the exact location of gestures and their nature. A recent study at Purdue University indicates that men and women who are purposefully touched on their hands, whether they are aware of it or not, tend to develop more positive feelings toward themselves. Also, a high sense of playfulness is attained among college students who are touched on the legs while touching of the hands communicates a loving gesture.

Generally speaking, we live in an impersonal world, observes Winter, where the lack of touching directly relates to our troubles. She believes that more awareness and communication will come with increased touching and increased understanding of our responses to it.

# chapter fourteen

# Self-Realization and Human Interaction through Touch

CARY L. COOPER AND DAVID BOWLES
*"Physical Encounter and Self-Disclosure"*

Among encounter and sensitivity training groups, body-touching exercises are often used as a technique to reduce barriers between the participants. Cooper and Bowles concerned themselves with such physical and body contact exercises and their relationship to self-disclosure. Their initial thesis was that such body contact in an encounter group tends to break down barriers and results in the participants' willingness to disclose more about themselves.

Twenty-seven undergraduate students in Southampton, England, volunteered to participate in a two-hour encounter session that was the basis of the study. Eighteen were randomly assigned to two experimental groups and nine to a control group.

From *Psychological Reports*, 33 (1973), 451-454.

It was determined that these volunteers did not differ significantly from the rest of the student body on two personality characteristics known to be related to self-disclosure—namely extraversion and neuroticism. Participants' self-disclosure ratings before and after the encounter group session were determined by self-report on Jourard's Self-Disclosure Scale. There was a significant difference in pre- and posttest scores for those who participated in the body contact exercises but not for the control group. The experimental group showed increased willingness to disclose themselves after the session.

Cooper and Bowles's findings support the belief held in the human potential movement that the elimination of touching taboos will help people disclose more of themselves to others. The researchers noted that this self-disclosure may be only temporary and may dissipate over a period of time. This time limitation, however, may not impede the attainment of the goal of an encounter group—namely, enhanced self-awareness gained through the experience of sharing in the encounter group itself.

F. B. Dresslar
*"Studies in the Psychology of Touch"*

In this article published in *The American Journal of Psychology* in 1894, Dresslar presents his opinions on the significance of touch in relation to other senses, and traces the impact of our tactile sensations not only on our mood and general temperament but also on the effectiveness of our communication.

A person is not considered abnormal if his or her hearing is indiscriminating. However, there may be some question regarding the same person if he or she cannot distinguish through touch thousands of variations in objects, location, quality, temperature, and so forth. The realm of touch puts us in contact with the most

From *The American Journal of Psychology*, VI, no. 3 (June 1894), 313-368.

important, permanent properties of things. Through touch we determine temperature, hardness, roughness, shape, and compressibility.

The "real world," according to Dresslar, is one we can touch. We may be persuaded that the objects we see before us are illusory, but if we are allowed to stretch out our hands and touch an object, we cease to doubt that it really exists. Other senses may falter or become useless, "but the conditions of touch remain so long as there is objective existence at all." Dresslar paraphrases Aristotle in saying that "we can have an animal without eyes, without the sense of smell, or taste, or hearing, but all must have the sense of touch."

Children learn the notion of otherness, separating the ego from the nonego, says Dresslar, by taking hold of an object external to themselves. If, in this experience, there were a single sensation or a set of sensations fused, children would grow up without the notion of otherness. The author asserts that in childhood, our senses are closer to us as we "feel the world." Feeling our feet in cool wet sand on a hot day is far more real than reading about it, seeing it in a movie, or even thinking about it. These semiconscious feelings from our skin have a significant effect upon our mood, temperament, and sense of ease. We reach our greatest sense of consciousness when we are fully aware of our external sense impressions.

"The *role* that touch plays in the expression of the emotions of love and friendship can scarcely be over-estimated. The psychological significance of this fact is seen in many words we use for friendship and love. The words, *attraction, affection,* and the phrase, *attached to,* illustrate this." Each of these words suggests the notion of being in contact with a loved one and implies a desire to be in dermal contact as a means of expressing friendship and love.

A common cultural pattern among almost all groups is seen

in the use of tactual expression in "their deepest and most fervent feelings of love and friendship" and in "their heartiest salutations and greetings." The reason we shake hands is not to confirm the absence of a dagger in the other's hand (a popular belief), but to show friendship. Grasping the hand gives us data concerning the person that is not available from any other source. The warmth, passivity, and type of grasp found in a handshake have a significant effect on how we perceive persons we meet.

Dresslar goes on to describe research done by others of his time regarding the sensitivity of the skin to the points of a compass as two distinct points. The ability to discriminate the two compass points varies for different parts of the body and among different persons. It was found that individuals could improve their discrimination through practice. It was also learned that improved two-point discrimination on a given part of the body through practice was also found on the symmetrical part on the other half of the body. However, there was no improvement through practice on the median line of the body between the shoulder blades. Dresslar describes his own series of experiments regarding the improvement of skin sensitivity for two-point discrimination.

JEFFREY D. FISHER, MARVIN RYTTING, AND RICHARD HESLIN
*"Hands Touching Hands: Affective and Evaluative Effects of an Interpersonal Touch"*

Fisher and his colleagues point to the growing interest among people, ranging from academicians to television producers, in human interaction and particularly in touch. "Go ahead and touch, go ahead and feel; reach out and see if what you

From *Sociometry*, 39 (1976), 416-421.

see is real," they quote from a popular children's television program. The message urges people to get beyond the point "when you were afraid to touch something beautiful."

The authors refer to the research on touch by Harlow (1971), Denenberg and Rosenberg (1967), Denenberg and Whimbey (1963), and Levine (1960). They found that early contact, touching, and handling are not only beneficial but essential to the intellectual, emotional, and social growth of animals. They also refer to Spitz (1946), who in a classic work wrote of the essential nature of early touching. The findings of Montagu (1971) and Morris (1973) concur with that theory, report the authors, revealing that tactile stimulation of infants is significant in their emotional, intellectual, and physiological development.

Fisher et al. explain that research appears both to confirm and deny the positive value of touching on adults. Positive effects of touch were found by Aguilera (1967), as it increased verbal communication and positively altered psychiatric patients' attitudes toward nurses. Self-disclosure of a client was increased through touching in counseling sessions, according to Pattison (1973).

Researchers finding a negative response included Walker (1971), Clarke (1971), and Poaster (1971). Whereas Walker found subjects generally uncomfortable in communications that included touching, Clark (studying levels of trust) and Poaster (studying empathy) found no significant differences in subjects who were touched and others who were not.

The authors give a detailed account of a study of momentary tactile contact among adult strangers at Purdue University. In this study, four library clerks either touched or did not touch the hand of students when returning their library card. This touching contact has a positive effect on the recipient's affective state and evaluation of the library clerks involved. This response occurred whether or not the touch was perceived. The design of the experiment is offered as a possible model for further studies.

MARK L. KNAPP
*"The Effects of Touching Behavior on Human Communication"*

This chapter in Knapp's book, *Nonverbal Communication in Human Interaction*, contains a valuable review and summarization of many of the recent studies pertaining to human touching. Knapp refers to various taxonomies and categorizations of touching behavior; individual researchers and writers use differing concepts as their organizing principles, such as the relative frequency of different types of touches, the degree of intimacy of the touch, the purpose of the touch, or the meaning of the touch.

Knapp reports on Bardeen's study, in which some persons were shown to prefer touch to visual and verbal communication (Bardeen, 1971).* Bardeen's subjects were led to believe that they were communicating with three different persons via three different modes. They actually interacted with only one person. The first mode was touch only while subjects were blindfolded; the second mode was visual only, and the third was verbal only. In reporting on the touch-only encounter, subjects used terms like "warm," "mature," "natural," "trustful," and "sensitive." They described the verbal-only communication as "artificial," "formal," "noncommunicative," and "distant." Visual-only communication was described as "arrogant," "comic," "artificial," and "childish."

Addressing the question of who touches whom, Knapp comments that in American society, touching is seen primarily as an extremely personal and intimate interaction. He adds that some parents teach their children not to touch. He cites some research

*J.B. Bardeen, "Interpersonal Perceptions Through the Tactile, Verbal, and Visual Modes," paper presented at ICA convention, Phoenix, 1971.

that describes situations in which people are more likely to touch. One of the places where the most touching behavior occurs seems to be at airports, particularly when someone is departing. In professional or job-related situations, it is typically the person of higher status who initiates a touching action; in such cases, men are the initiators more often than women.

Knapp reports on a study conducted in 1976 that shows a trend toward more adult touching by comparison with a similar study ten years earlier. Adult males and females in the later study were touching opposite-sex friends more frequently and in more intimate places, such as hips, thighs, stomachs, and chests.

Another researcher, Morris (1973), concentrated on one specific type of touching—the embrace. He observed the full embrace in touching activities in American society. It ranged from a gesture between lovers to one between friends and relatives, athletes, or any variety of persons at times of triumph, reunion, greeting, and farewell. Partial embraces, involving side-to-side contact and one arm around the other person's body, are six times as likely to occur among adults in public as full embraces, discovered Morris. The partial embrace most commonly given by males is the shoulder embrace in which the hand is placed on the same-sex friend's far shoulder. In the United States, he adds, hand-holding is seen infrequently between persons of the same sex. Special occasions calling for this gesture are generally as curtain calls or in times of joint victory.

Research on self-touching shows that acutely depressed patients demonstrate a wide range of such actions. Self-touching also occurs among others, however, and expresses itself in activities such as scratching, rubbing, picking, wiping the body with the hands, covering the mouth and ears in a way to reduce input, and the self-intimacies of holding one's own hands, hugging one's own legs, and masturbating. Freedman's work (1972) as well as Morris's research seems to indicate that we all touch ourselves in various ways, to ease our fears, particularly in the absence of loved ones.

Knapp reports on a study by Jourard (1966) that documents a wide range of touching behavior demonstrated by couples in cafes in various parts of the world. Couples in cafes in London, England, and Gainesville, Florida, did much less touching in an hour than couples in Paris, France, and San Juan, Puerto Rico. This study and others indicate that touching is experienced in some cultures more than in others. Although our puritanical history has placed us among the nontouchers, it has been shown that American touching activity is greater than that in certain other cultures such as Japan. Perhaps the so-called noncontact culture of American society is changing; certainly there is a considerable degree of variation in this regard among the various subgroups within it.

In summarizing his findings, Knapp notes:

> In some cases, touching is the most effective method for communicating; in others, it can elicit negative or hostile reactions. The meanings we attach to touching behavior vary according to what body part is touched, how long the touch lasts, the strength of the touch, the method of the touch (for example, open or closed fist) and the frequency of the touch. Touch also means different things in different environments (institutions, airports, and so on) and with communicators varying in age, sex, and stage of relationship.
>
> Touching behavior can be used to communicate interpersonal attitudes (such as dominance, affection, and the like).

NORMAN M. LOBSENZ
*"The Loving Message in a Touch"*

Helen Keller's words, "Paradise is attained by touch," best exemplify Lobsenz's thesis. He believes that interpersonal relationships offer a multitude of opportunities to communicate

From *Woman's Day*, February 1970, pp. 132-134. Copyright © 1970 by Norman Lobsenz.

**193**

through touching, but the opportunities are realized infrequently except in times of crisis. At critical times, humans rely on touching to communicate emotional support, caring affections, encouragement, and tenderness. At other times they overlook touching's potential and replace it with words, allowing closeness to be replaced with distance.

The author maintains that the benefits of touch are realized very early in life. Touching fosters growth in infants and children; youngsters who receive the most physical contact from parents or parent substitutes indisputably attain the highest IQs and walk and talk earlier than others. But ironically, children soon learn that touching is not nice; they must not do it. An Anglo-Saxon cultural heritage communicates in many ways a disapproval of touching because of its ingrained sensual connotation. Youngsters grow into adults who shy away from touching for the sake of communication, resisting touch even by their own sex partners.

Since touching in our culture primarily suggests either combat or sexual activity, we need new rules in order to change our behavior from nontouching to self-rewarding touching. Suggestions are as follows:

1. Learn to "read" the appropriate times and places when others will be receptive to your contact.
2. Communicate to friends, family, and associates that you wish to extend your sense of communication by touching.
3. Explain changes in your simplest acts of touching such as replacing a greeting handshake with an embrace.
4. Touch sincerely; don't disguise the meaning of a touch.
5. Touch for the purpose of communicating, not to control or demand.
6. Learn that different kinds of touching mean different things and that touching per se does not always reflect a sexual interest.

Lobsenz suggests that touching is a sharing, an exchange that allows us to continue to grow in our humanness. He offers the foregoing rules as guidelines to facilitate this sharing.

**194**

J. Lomranz and A. Shapira
*"Communicative Patterns of Self-Disclosure and Touching Behavior"*

The writers explain that touching is a form of communication that discloses feelings, emotions, and personality. Both self-disclosure and touching behavior are components of interpersonal communication. They hypothesized that individuals who demonstrate a high degree of self-disclosure will also be high in touching behavior, on the condition that their cultural environment supports touching behaviors.

Lomranz and Shapira conducted a study of ninety-five male and ninety-five female middle-class Israeli high school students, ages seventeen to nineteen, in Tel Aviv. They evaluated the subjects' self-disclosure and touching behavior by means of two standard questionnaires. They found a high positive correlation between self-disclosure and touching behavior. Also, men were found to exhibit significantly more touching than women. Women demonstrated higher ratings of self-disclosure than men, although this difference only approached the significant level.

Lomranz and Shapira also found that most touching takes place between opposite-sex close friends. Significantly, self-disclosure and touching rated higher among peer friends of the same sex or the opposite sex than with the subjects' parents.

The authors reported that this desire to touch and to communicate through touch originates with newborn children. Through touching, babies learn what is and is not a part of their bodies. As they grow, their attitudes toward touching vary for many reasons, one of which is their cultural environment. There are contact and noncontact cultures, they say, and the United States definitely qualifies in the noncontact category. When compared with American males, Middle Eastern males tend to be much more permissive about touching behavior.

From *Journal of Psychology*/Journal Press, August 5, 1974, pp. 223-227.

John McLaughlin
*"Sense Communication"*

There has been a phenomenal growth in the popular interest in sense communication in America and abroad. Emotional starvation results from taboos against touch! Claims like these inspired overly zealous individuals to roam the streets in Notting Hill, England, reaching out to touch as many persons as possible. Most of the recipients reacted to the touching with expressions of astonishment and fear. The only exceptions were West Indians and persons of Latin extraction, who expressed enjoyment of the contact.

The author explains that sense experience has a high association with sexuality, mostly attributable to the touch component. The simultaneous upswing in sense communication and sexual experience frequently makes it difficult to distinguish between the two—thus the misgivings of passersby in Notting Hill!

The increase in awareness of the senses does not suggest a general moral decay, McLaughlin reassures us. Conversely, there is much evidence in our culture to suggest that our moral consciousness is more profound and widespread than ever.


David N. Walker
*"A Dyadic Interaction Model for Nonverbal Touching Behavior in Encounter Groups"*

Walker studied dyadic interaction (interaction between persons in pairs) to determine if nonverbal touching exercises foster interpersonal openness. The purpose of his study was to shed some light on the controversy between encounter group trainers and their critics regarding the effectiveness of nonverbal touching

McLaughlin from *America*, June 21, 1969, pp. 716-717.

This paraphrase of "A Dyadic Interaction Model for Nonverbal Touching in Encounter Groups" by David N. Walker is reprinted from *Small Group Behavior*, 6, no. 3 (August 1975), 308-324.

techniques in encounter groups. Critics have suggested that such techniques foster defensiveness, produce stress, and are psychologically disturbing to participants.

Walker hypothesized that (1) in general, people are uncomfortable in nonverbal touching interaction; (2) there are sex differences in nonverbal touching behavior, and these are affected by whether the partner is of the same of the opposite sex; (3) as nonverbal touching continues, openness to it increases; and (4) personality characteristics affect openness to touching.

The study involved 180 unmarried university students in thirty dyads of each of the following types: male–male, female–female, male-female. Subjects were rated on their openness to touching at three points in the course of seven nonverbal touching exercises. These consisted of such activities as head touching, shoulder slapping, back-to-back touching, and a palm dance. The subjects also rated their moods before and after the touching exercises.

The first hypothesis and the critics' views of the negative effects of nonverbal touching interaction on participants were substantiated by the study. Causal factors for low openness and discomfort in touching interactions, according to the author, were as follows: (1) subjects were strangers to each other; (2) subjects knew they were being observed; and (3) subjects viewed intimate touching, under these conditions, as not acceptable in our society.

Walker found that females were more open to touching in all-female dyads than were males in all-male dyads. This is explained by the sexual link to touching in our society. Specifically, in our culture, females are more likely to touch each other than are males. Walker speculated on the differences in openness to touching in male–male and female–female dyads, saying that attitudes may vary because of differences in attitudes toward homosexuality. Whereas men fear the stigma of homosexuality, women remain relatively unconcerned about it and are consequently less threatened by touching other women. He adds that nonverbal touching can successfully foster openness when (1) cultural taboos against touching are relaxed and (2) participants feel they can trust group members to be caring individuals.

Although the raters found the subjects more open to touching at the end of the session than at the beginning, the subjects saw themselves as less open. At the end of the nonverbal touching interactions, subjects felt more anxious, more distant, more depressed, more guilty, more angry, less affectionate, less joyful, less relaxed, and less sexually aroused.

Regarding the significance of personality types on openness to touch, the author concluded that the most appropriate use of nonverbal touching methods is found when the participants do not have guilt feelings about sex, when they exhibit a strong need for affection, and when they demonstrate a sexually noncallous feeling toward others. The overall results of the study, however, seem to indicate that even when sensitive trainers and certain personality types are involved in the groups, nonverbal touching techniques are, at best, a dubious method for increasing openness.

# chapter fifteen

# The Place of Touch in Physical and Emotional Health

IRENE MORTENSON BURNSIDE
*"Touching Is Talking"*

"A simple, warm, human gesture like a hand on his shoulder can do more to help an elderly regressed patient respond than many sophisticated techniques," claims nursing researcher, Irene Burnside. In 1973 Burnside substituted "touch therapy" for "food therapy" in group sessions treating elderly regressed patients when she observed "touch hunger" in a patient who pulled her head down and kissed her tenderly on the cheek as Burnside held her hand.

Bolstered by McCorkle's study of nurses' successful efforts at conveying messages to patients through a caring touch, the author used touching in an attempt to encourage some behaviors and modify others. She sought to discourage the behaviors of babbling, withdrawal, inappropriate replies, exhibitionism, and refusal to make eye contact; she sought to encourage laughter, smiles, spontaneous behavior (e.g., clapping to music), displays of affection, interest in clothes and food, and eye contact, and interpersonal touching behavior.

To greet and say good-bye to every patient at each meeting, she used an Indian handshake—one hand placed in theirs and her other hand on top of the two clasped hands. She also put her hand on the patients' shoulders when she spoke to them. She touched the men as she gave them cigars, and she touched the ambulatory patients by dancing with them.

Her efforts seemed to take effect. She began to observe some touching among patients, less hallucinating, response to music, and increased eye contact. Ironically, after the group meeting when, for the first time, all the patients squeezed one another's hands to say good-bye, one of the patients died.

Burnside saw hope in touch therapy, a method that seemed to work where technology, drugs, and doctors seemed to fail. She had made a difference in the life of one man very near death and hoped to continue to make a difference in the lives of more elderly patients.

ARTHUR BURTON AND LOUIS G. HELLER
*"The Touching of the Body"*

A frantic search has begun in this century, a search for the body in its totality and in its various parts. Burton and Heller explain how Western humanity has become increasingly estranged from the body. We are less aware and less accepting of our bodies than Asians are, depending more on cosmetics and prostheses.

From *Psychoanalytic Review*, 51 (Spring 1964), 122-134.

The authors trace the origin of the taboo against touching the body and review the taboo's influence on schizophrenic patients and the practice of psychotherapy.

The authors explain that humankind has selected one sense mode over another, and the selection has been reinforced by culture. Thus, the visual, auditory, and gustatory senses have overshadowed the tactual and olfactory senses. The tactual sense, serving to locate a person in time and space, remains essential, they add, and potentially can help people to establish a foundation for higher-order operations.

People continue to resist touch, however. One reason for this, they say, is that touch forces us to view the finitude of our bodies. Even in the medical profession, workers are reluctant to touch the aging person, as it calls to mind their own mortality. "The body is what is born and what dies, and this is disturbing," the authors point out. This interferes with our natural and basic need for human touch.

The tactual sense of an unborn child is his or her orientation to the mother and to life. After birth, the infant still craves this feeling of oneness; gaining as much psychologically from the touch of the mother's breast as he or she does physically from the food received.

A similar craving for touch can be seen in developing children. Uninhibited toddlers find that they must abruptly curtail their habits of easy touching; the taboo of touching comes into play to fetter their spontaneous gestures and cast suspicion on any touching they might receive. As a result, many youngsters with problems provoke punishment out of a desire to be touched, even though the end result will certainly cause pain. Pain may then become valued as the means for physical contact and confirmation to the child that he or she does indeed exist.

The authors compare schizophrenic patients to children who are in need of being fondled. These patients seek human relatedness, and according to several psychotherapists, some limited form of body contact should be used in their treatment.

Burton and Heller explain that regressed schizophrenic and geriatric patients want to touch others "to reassure themselves of their continuity and existence." An anticipation of decline and death motivates them to cling tactually to the world and to their unconscious remembrances of maternal touching.

Unfortunately, contend the writers, psychoanalytic psychotherapists today have a fear of touching their patients, referring them to physicians for physical examination and treatment. They recommend that psychotherapists try to create a sense of freedom to touch if it is needed. They indicate that shaking hands is the first stage of establishing rapport. It is a culturally desexualized act to acknowledge the meeting of two people. Clasping the hands can bring a warmer, longer, and sometimes more intense awareness of contact, with the suggestion that the encounter will bring fulfillment. Of course, doctors are reminded to proceed cautiously, remaining aware of the patient's interpretation of their gestures.

MARGARET K. DEWEVER
*"Nursing Home Patients' Perception of Nurses' Affective Touching"*

DeWever explains that nurses use active touching of patients to communicate empathy and sympathy; yet few researchers have studied the patient's passive response to touching. Research does show that affective touching enhances interaction between nurse and patient. DeWever concentrates on the gestures that foster interaction.

She discovered that because of an elaborate and unwritten touching code in our society, patients often misinterpret the meaning of touching by nurses. They have programmed *sensory* responses, dictated to a large extent by their cultural background.

From *Journal of Psychology*/Journal Press, 1977, pp. 163-171.

The vehicle for the cultural rules that limit touching is usually one's parents, explains DeWever.

In North America, she says, we touch each other basically in intimate relationships, equating touching with sexuality. Within this pattern, there are variations on the theme. Factors that influence differences are (1) family ties, (2) social status, (3) age, (4) sex, (5) loneliness, and (6) illness. Families usually develop their own peculiar code of touching conduct. DeWever found, but all individuals appear to crave more touching during periods of illness and loneliness.

Sex and social relationships also govern our touching and reactions to it. According to Jourard and Rubin (1968), more touching takes place between friends of the opposite sex than between same-sex friends, and according to Henley (1973), persons who actively touch are of a higher social status than persons who cuddle to touches. Henley's conclusion is that recipients of affective touching are of a lower or submissive status.

Investigating patients' perceived comfort or discomfort in response to touch, DeWever studied the influence of age, sex, and patient classification on the receiver's response. Seven modalities were used: (1) nurse's hand touching the patient's face; (2) nurse's hand on patient's shoulder; (3) nurse's hand touching patient's head; (4) nurse's arm around patient's shoulder; (5) nurse's hand on patient's hand; and (6) nurse holding patient's hand.

A majority of the patients who participated enjoyed affective touching by nurses. However, about half the patients felt some discomfort, and approximately 2 percent of them felt uncomfortable about all affective touching.

The interest in and need for touch increases with the age of the patient, observed DeWever, and affective touching by male nurses brings more discomfort to female patients than touching by female nurses. The greatest discomfort in female patients was associated with touching from older male nurses.

The author concluded that (1) placing the nurse's arm around the patient's shoulders caused the greatest amount of discomfort in the greatest number of patients; (2) the nurse's hand touching the patient's arm was accepted as the most comfortable affective behavior; and (3) an older female nurse's touch to the face was well accepted by nearly all patients. DeWever's findings imply that nurses can use selective techniques to comfort their patients through touch.

BETTY SUE JOHNSON
*"The Meaning of Touch in Nursing"*

According to Johnson, among the medical and helping professions, nursing necessitates the most direct contact and touching of patients. How nurses communicate through touch is directly related to both their own *and* the patients' attitudes toward touch. She states that touching is a vital part of our social interaction and communication. As infants, we rely almost exclusively on touch as a means of communication. As adults, we respond to touch differently.

The variations in interpretation of touching by adults and their feelings of comfort with it are related to the individuals' experiences with touching while growing up, and are dictated by both their age group and current cultural patterns. The author explains that certain persons use touch as a way of initiating verbal exchange. Others use touch to emphasize verbal communication. In many cultures, such as those in Latin America, the use of touch along with verbal communication is rather universal. Other people tend to feel uncomfortable when touched in any way. Thus, nurses need to recognize that their patients may have different levels of receptiveness to touch and interpretations of it.

Some basic concepts should be considered when using touch as a form of communication:

1. Nonverbal communication, especially touch, has the potential for being the most meaningful form of communication.
2. Touch, as a form of nonverbal communication, is of primary importance, especially when we wish to communicate feelings and attitudes.
3. Touch improves communication more effectively when it is accompanied by corresponding verbal behavior.
4. When touch and verbal behavior convey different messages, communication is open to possible conflict. Receivers of this type of communication must decide if they will respond to the touch or to the verbal cue.
5. Touch messages rely on the subjective interpretation of the recipient and have greater potential for misunderstanding than verbal communication.
6. The "when and how" of touch will have an effect upon verbal communication.
7. When touch becomes part of an interaction, it is vital to explain the reasons for and nature of the touching.

Johnson cautions nurses to be sure that the verbal messages and touch messages they communicate are not contradictory.

DOLORES KRIEGER
*"Therapeutic Touch: The Imprimatur of Nursing"*

The act of therapeutic touch is "absurdly simple," explains Dolores Krieger: an individual lays his or her hands on or close to the body of the ill person for ten or fifteen minutes. It is essential that the "healer" has the strong intention to help or heal the ill person and that the "healer" possesses a healthy body. Faith on the part of the ill person is not a requisite.

Laying on of hands is an ancient practice that is depicted in the remains of the earliest cultures. It has been practiced throughout centuries of human history up to the present day. Krieger has found insights into this practice in the literature of Eastern religions. In Sanskrit, there is a word for a state of matter connoting vitality or vigor—*prana; prana* is intrinsic to what we call the oxygen molecule. The healthy person has an overabundance of *prana* and the ill person, a lack. In the laying on of hands, the healthy person wills to transfer *prana* to the ill person.

Krieger's article summarizes studies on therapeutic touch conducted by Bernard Grad in the early 1960s. His experiments involved the effect of therapeutic touch on mice and barley seeds. In the late sixties, Sr. M. Justa Smith conducted studies on the effect of therapeutic touch on enzymes.

Krieger herself studied the effects of therapeutic touch given by a noted healer, Estebany, to ill persons. She hypothesized that therapeutic touch would increase the hemoglobin content in the blood of an ill person. Hemoglobin is the pigment of the red blood cells that carries oxygen to the body tissues. She conducted a pilot study in 1971 and subsequent fuller studies in 1972 and 1973. The results supported her hypothesis to a .01 level of significance in the first two cases and to a .001 level of significance in the third study.

In 1974, Krieger conducted another study in which nurses in New York used therapeutic touch on hospital patients. The findings of this study also support her hypothesis.

Krieger explains that all people have had extremely meaningful and personal experiences with touch, beginning with the stimulation of the skin in the birth canal. The touch-healing process is simply another meaningful touch experience that is within the natural potential of physically healthy persons who are strongly motivated to help sick persons.

DOLORES KRIEGER
*"Therapeutic Touch"*

In this article, Dolores Krieger reviews the history of
research conducted by B. Grad (1964) and Sr. M. Justa Smith
(1972) on therapeutic touch since 1960 and the related concept of
*prana* in Eastern culture.

Therapeutic touch, also known as laying on of hands, "is a
uniquely human act of concern of one individual for another,"
she explains. Krieger reports on observing Oskar Estebany, a
well-known healer who uses treatment characterized by touching
another with the intent of helping or healing the person so touched.
Estebany's technique requires no fancy maneuvers. He simply
sits quietly next to the person under treatment and lays his hands
on the patient's body for twenty to twenty-five minutes in an area
he considers important to the patient. Krieger was surprised to
find through follow-up reports that a "greater than chance
number of these patients got well."

In her desire to learn how and why therapeutic touch works,
Krieger turned to the technique of Kirlian photography, which
reportedly "demonstrates some kind of energy emission." Two
Kirlian photographs were taken of her hands. The first
photography showed her hands as they were under normal circumstances; the second photograph showed her hands in their
position of practicing therapeutic touch. Very few seconds elapsed
between the first and second photographs. A comparison of the
photographs shows a distinct change in energy level between the
first photograph of the resting hand and the second photograph of
the hand simulating therapeutic touch.

Concluding that an alteration in energy level associated with
therapeutic touch can be brought about at will, Krieger

From *Nursing Times*, April 15, 1976, pp. 572-574.

postulates that it could be studied under laboratory conditions and subjected to the rigors of scientific methodology. She suggests that such a study would be valuable research in nursing.

Krieger has set up a course at the master's level at New York University, where she is a professor, to teach graduate students of nursing the process of therapeutic touch and to help develop a theoretical basis for understanding how it works.

RUTH MCCORKLE
*"Effects of Touch on Seriously Ill Patients"*

McCorkle reviews the literature that describes the important role of touch in the womb, during birth, and throughout life. She notes that an adult in an unfamiliar situation (such as in a hospital) unconsciously tends to revert to earlier, more primitive modes of human interaction, such as touch. She cites the work of Elisabeth Kübler-Ross, who has found touch to be the most meaningful mode of communication with seriously ill persons, particularly with those who have accepted their condition of terminal illness. Other research has shown, on the other hand, that health team personnel tend to touch patients in fair and good condition 70 percent more often than those more seriously ill.

In her own research, McCorkle proposed to examine the effects of touch on seriously ill patients. To do this, she compared the responses of seriously ill patients who received verbal communication and touching to the responses of those who received verbal communication without being touched. She hypothesized: "Touching and verbally stimulating a seriously ill patient will produce an increase in the number of positive acceptance responses." She devised a multifaceted method of measuring positive acceptance responses, including observation of behavioral reactions (e.g., eye contact, facial expressions, body movements) by two persons other than the investigator, the patient's own subjective reaction elicited by an observer after the interaction, and, for some patients, changes in heart rate and rhythm. The subjects were sixty seriously ill hospitalized patients, divided into experimental and control groups.

McCorkle's hypothesis was supported by patients' "facial expression" responses but not by the other behaviors analyzed. The majority of patients in both the experimental and control groups said the nurse was interested in them. An interesting observation was that during the postinteraction questioning, many of the patients who had been touched by the investigator readily touched the person interviewing them.

McCorkle concludes that nurses can establish rapport with seriously ill patients in a short period of time. Touching the patients is a factor demonstrating that nurses care for them. However, understanding the effects of touching is only a beginning in using communication skills with patients.

JOYCE E. PATTISON
*"Effects of Touch on Self-Exploration and the Therapeutic Relationship"*

Touching as a means of communication is assuming an ever-increasing role in present-day therapeutic practices, contends Joyce Pattison. Research suggests that even a single touch can bring about a feeling of caring and acceptance. Many authors contend that touching a patient facilitates mutual openness and unreserve. Others warn that touching may be harmful.

Pattison reports on the findings of Aguilera's study on verbal gestures between nurses and psychiatric patients that showed

From *Journal of Consulting and Clinical Psychology*, 40, no. 2 (1973), 170-175.

that after eight days of treatment, touching gestures increased verbal communication (Aguilera, 1967). Significant positive correlations also exist, she reports, between self-disclosure and touching in cases of males disclosing to males and females disclosing to males, according to Jourard and Rubin (1968). Thus we may assume that touch is a factor in the establishment of a relationship and in the exploration of the self. Research shows that relationship and self-exploration are related to positive therapeutic outcome in psychotherapy. Also, the conditions for a good therapeutic relationship include warmth and positive regard; both of these seem to be related to touch.

Pattison conducted a study to test the "relationship between touching as a therapeutic technique and two process variables—self-exploration and perception of relationship." Twenty female undergraduate students were the subjects of her study; ten were assigned to a male counselor, ten to a female counselor. Each counselor followed a touch procedure designated by Pattison with five clients and a no-touch procedure with the other five.

Clients receiving touch treatment engaged in more self-exploration than clients receiving no-touch treatment, to a .01 level of significance. Touch, however, had no significant relationship to counselors' or clients' perceptions of the relationship offered by the counselor.

Pattison's findings demonstrate the significance of touching in counseling. She leaves her readers with these compelling questions: What is it that touch is providing the client? Is it safety? Is it reward? Is it a breakdown of defensive postures? Does touching bring about higher or lower anxiety? Also, under what conditions should we touch for maximum effectiveness? Upon what occasions, for what lengths of time, and in what locations? What sex differences need to be considered? Although opinions vary on touching, "there seems to be agreement that the nature of the touch and the nature of the relationship are important variables."

TONIE PRESTON
*"When Words Fail"*

Preston describes organic brain syndrome patients who were unable to communicate verbally and yet responded to non-verbal cues communicated through facial expressions and touch.

Preston observed that an eighty-year-old patient with organic brain syndrome returned to semi-reality and ate and enjoyed his food without babbling, when nurses held his hand during meals. When the nurses repeatedly placed their arms around another patient's shoulders, while showing sympathetic facial expressions, the patient began to respond with hand gestures; he was unable to communicate with words.

According to Preston, non-verbal communication appears to be automatic, much like the conditioned responses learned in childhood. She adds that, in senile patients, conditioned responses remain long after more complex voice communications are lost. These patients automatically reach out to show affection, even though they cannot verbalize it. At the same time, they can be restrained through non-verbal cues learned in early childhood. A grasp around their wrists, with light force, tells them their behavior is unacceptable or may result in some harm just as it tells youngsters who have learned the cue.

In explaining this phenomenon, researchers say that "Verbal and nonverbal symbols do not relate to the same sensory modalities." Nonverbal language takes on more importance when verbal languages fail. She emphasizes that, for the senile patient, nonverbal messages learned as a child may be the only means of exchange in interpersonal relationships, and they can greatly help improve his or her comfort in old age.

WILBUR H. WATSON
*"The Meanings of Touch: Geriatric Nursing"*

Touching is an intentional act that can be instrumental or expressive, says Watson. An instrumental act in nursing is touching for the purpose of helping, such as lifting or assisting a patient. This type of touching is used primarily by health professionals. Expressive touching, on the other hand, communicates a feeling. It is spontaneous and is not usually considered a requirement in institutional relationships.

The author shows, however, that the two types of touching overlap in nursing. Nurses generally do not remain completely impersonal; they maintain a variety of feelings in response to their patients, offering selective touching. The variables are (1) parts of the patient's body to be touched, (2) sex and social status of the patient, and (3) personal appearance of the patient.

One study showed that nurses preferred young schizophrenic patients to older depressed patients. The younger group responded most actively to touching gestures, becoming more open and cooperative.

Watson also emphasizes the direct relationship between the sex and rank of the nurse, on one hand, and the type and location of the touching on the other. He found that the higher-ranking nurses use expressive touching more than lower-ranking nurses. Correspondingly, lower-ranking orderlies touch patients less frequently than nurses. The author also notes that male and female nurses systematically refrain from touching or looking at the

From *Journal of Communication*, Summer 1975, pp. 104-112.

genitals of their patients, a definite taboo in their profession; neither do they touch the scalps of opposite-sex patients, another taboo area. The mouth is touched only in administering medicine, and the head remains out-of-bounds most of the time.

He notes that touching activities increase over the parts of the body greater in distance from those parts considered taboo. Since low-ranking individuals are confined by the most taboos, it is not surprising that they are most apt to select the hand–wrist area for contacting patients.

Watson explains that patients receiving the least attention in institutions are males with severe impairments. It is clear that this unfortunate lack of touching is due to cultural codes that limit touching activities on the basis of sex and to the lack of attractiveness that results from their impairment.

LORI J. ZEFRON
*"the history of the laying-on of hands in nursing"*

Lori Zefron believes that nurses can help patients by using the power of therapeutic touch. She outlines the history of laying on of hands and relates it to the nurse's role.

Zefron speculates that the first recognition of the healing power of touch could well have occurred among ancient cave dwellers. Feeling compassion for a sick friend, they might have placed a hand on their companion's hot brow and then attributed the ensuing recovery to their touch.

The Tasadays, a Philippine Stone Age tribe found in the Mindanao jungle in 1966, exhibit a need for touching as a means of expression among fellow tribe members. Adults and children have been observed huddled together in tactile unity. Instinctively, we have known that human beings, in order to survive and attain

From *Nursing Forum*, Vol. XIV, 4 (1975), 350-363.

good health, need to be touched, stroked, and cuddled. Observing the Tasadays gives us a reasonable scientific basis for our views on the essential value of touch to life. In our culture, however, we learn to depend less on touch activities to relay messages of caring and understanding and to call upon words to express these ideas.

Many researchers report the beneficial effects of touch in modern life. Zefron relates one incident concerning a seriously ill cardiac patient. The patient's scope monitor heightened with erratic activity when his wife came to his bedside, but the heart behavior smoothed out after she gently stroked his body, legs, and head.

Zefron refers to the laying on of hands in the New Testament. She finds it significant that there are more accounts of Jesus healing the physically sick through touch than of him forgiving sins. Dr. Jim Knightlinger, a pathologist who prays with the incurably ill, is studying "auras" found on the hands of persons who reportedly have healed others upon whom they have laid their hands. Auras, in some circles, may be called *prana* or magnetic fielding. There appears to be a therapeutic "something" that can be transferred from one loving person to another. Jesus called it the power of God. In Luke 8:46, Jesus is reported to have stopped the twelve years of bleeding of a woman who touched His robe. He observed that someone had deliberately touched Him as "He felt the healing power go from Him."

Zefron complains that medical doctors have been resistant to the activities of healers, as the doctors feel that they alone have knowledge of the healing arts. The author reiterates, however, that nurses have a commitment to healing. Their art is one of caring, she says, and caring and loving are the same. She pleads with other nurses to lay hands on their patients and let the healing power pour through.

# Bibliography

ADLER, SOL, *The Non-Verbal Child*. Springfield, Ill.: Charles C Thomas, 1975.

AGUILERA, D. C., "Relationships Between Physical Contact and Verbal Interaction in Nurses and Patients," *Journal of Psychiatric Nursing*, 5 (1967), 5-21.

ALLEN. G., "Hate Therapy-Sensitivity Training for Planned Change," *Congressional Record—House* (December 12, H16781-16785), 1967.

ARGYLE, M. *Bodily Communication*. New York: University Press, 1975.

BARDEEN, J. P., "Interpersonal Perception Through the Tactile, Verbal, and Visual Modes," paper presented at the convention of the International Communication Association, Phoenix, 1971.

BUISSERET, PAUL, "The Six Senses," *Nursing Mirror Supplement*, January 26, 1978, pp. iii-iv.

BURNSIDE, IRENE MORTENSON, "Touching Is Talking," *American Journal of Nursing*, Vol. 73, No. 12 (Dec. 1973), 2060-2063.

BURTON, ARTHUR, AND LOUIS G. HELLER, "The Touching of the Body," *Psychoanalytic Review*, Vol. 51 (Spring 1964), 122-134.

CLARKE, J. F., "Some Effects of Nonverbal Activities and Group Discussion on Inter-Personal Trust Development in Small Groups," doctoral dissertation, Arizona State University. Ann Arbor, Mich.: University Microfilms No. 71-18 (1971), 955.

COOPER, CARY L., AND DAVID BOWLES, "Physical Encounter and Self-Disclosure," *Psychological Reports*, Vol. 33 (1973), 451-454.

DANCOFF, JUDITH, "Beyond Sex: Can Women and Men Be Just Friends?" *Mademoiselle*, Dec. 1975, pp. 80, 81.

DAVIDSON, PHILIP W., AND TERESA T. WHITSON, "Haptic Equivalence Matching of Curvature by Blind and Sighted Humans," *Journal of Experimental Psychology*, Vol. 102, No. 4 (1974), 687-690.

DENENBERG, V. H., AND A. E. WHIMBEY, "Behavior of Adult Rats Is Modified by the Experiences Their Mothers Had as Infants," *Science*, 142 (1963), 1192-1193.

DENENBERG, V. H., AND K. M. ROSENBERG, "Nongenetic Transmission of Information," *Nature*, 216 (1967), 549-550.

DEWEVER, MARGARET K., "Nursing Home Patients' Perception of Nurses' Affective Touching," *Journal of Psychology*, Vol. 96, No. 2 (1977), 163-171.

DRESSLAR, F. B., "Studies in the Psychology of Touch," *The American Journal of Psychology*, Vol. VI, No. 3 (June 1894), 313-368.

DURBIN, KAREN, "Beyond Sex: The Need to Touch," *Mademoiselle*, Dec. 1975, pp. 78-79.

FISHER, JEFFREY D., MARVIN RYTTING, AND RICHARD HESLIN, "Hands Touching Hands: Affective and Evaluative Effects of an Interpersonal Touch," *Sociometry*, Vol. 39 (1976), 416-421.

FREEDMAN, N., "The Analysis of Movement Behavior during the Clinical Interview," in A.W. Siegman and B. Pope (eds.), *Studies in Dyadic Communication*. New York: Pergamon, 1972.

GALTON, LAWRENCE, "For Mother and Child—Closer Encounters," *Parade*, Oct. 1, 1978, pp. 5-8.

GIBSON, JAMES J., "Observations on Active Touch," *Psychological Review*, Vol. 69, No. 6 (Nov. 1962), 477-491.

GRAD, BERNARD, "A Telekinetic Effect on Plant Growth," *International Journal of Parapsychology, 6* (1964), 473-498.

GRAVES, DOROTHY, "Right from the Start," *The PTA Magazine*, May 1969, pp. 22-24.

HARLOW, H., ed., *Learning of Love*. New York: Albion Publishing, 1971.

HENLEY, N. M., "The Politics of Touch," in P. Brown, ed., *Radical Psychology*. New York: Harper & Row, 1973.

HOLLENDER, MARC H., "The Need or Wish to Be Held," *Archives of General Psychiatry*, Vol. 22 (May 1970), 445-453.

HOLLENDER, MARC H., LESTER LUBORSKY, AND THOMAS J. SCARAMELLA, "Body Contact and Sexual Enticement," *Archives of General Psychiatry*, Vol. 20 (Feb. 1969), 188-191.

JOHNSON, BETTY SUE, "The Meaning of Touch in Nursing," *Nursing Outlook*, Feb. 1965, pp. 59-60.

JOURARD, S. M., "An Exploratory Study of Body-Accessibility," *British Journal of Social & Clinical Psychology*, 5 (1966), 221-231.

JOURARD, S. M., AND J. E. RUBIN, "Self-Disclosure and Touching: A Study of Two Modes of Interpersonal Encounter and Their Interrelation," *Journal of Humanistic Psychology*, Vol. VIII (1968), 39-48.

KALISH, RICHARD A., *The Psychology of Human Behavior*. Belmont, Calif.: Wadsworth, 1967.

KINSEY, ALFRED, *Sexual Behavior in the Human Female*. Philadelphia: Saunders, 1953.

KNAPP, MARK L., "The Effects of Touching Behavior on Human Communication," in *Nonverbal Communication in Human Interaction* (2nd ed.), Chap. 7, pp. 242-262. New York: Holt, Rinehart, & Winston, 1978.

KOCH, S., "The Image of Man Implicit in Encounter Group Theory," *Journal of Humanistic Psychology*, 11, 2 (1971), pp. 109-128.

KOSNIK, ANTHONY, et al., Commissioned by the Catholic Theological Society of America, *Human Sexuality: New Directions in American Catholic Thought: A Study*. New York: Paulist Press, 1977.

KRIEGER, DOLORES, "Therapeutic Touch: The Imprimatur of Nursing," *American Journal of Nursing*, May 1975, pp. 784-787.

KRIEGER, DOLORES, "Therapeutic Touch," *Nursing Times*, April 15, 1976, pp. 572-574.

LANDRIGAN, DAVID T., AND G. ALFRED FORSYTH, "Regulation and Production of Movement Effects in Exploration-Recognition Performance," *Journal of Experimental Psychology*, Vol. 103, No. 6 (1974), 1124-1130.

LEVINE, S., "Stimulation in Infancy," *Scientific American*, 202 (1960), 80-86.

LOBSENZ, NORMAN M., "The Loving Message in a Touch," *Woman's Day*, Feb. 1970, p. 30.

LOMRANZ, J.,AND A. SHAPIRA, "Communicative Patterns of Self-Disclosure and Touching Behavior," *Journal of Psychology*, Vol. 88, No. 2 (August 5, 1974), 223-227.

MASTERS, WILLIAM H., AND VIRGINIA E. JOHNSON in association with Robert J. Levin. *The Pleasure Bond: A New Look at Sexuality and Commitment*. Boston: Little, Brown and Co., 1970.

MCCORKLE, RUTH, "Effects of Touch on Seriously Ill Patients," *Nursing Research*, Vol. 23, No. 2 (March-April 1974), 125-132.

MCLAUGHLIN, JOHN, "Sense Communication," *America*, June 21, 1969, pp. 716-717.

MONTAGU, ASHLEY. *Touching: The Human Significance of the Skin*. New York: Columbia University Press, 1971.

MORRIS, DESMOND, ed., *Intimate Behavior*. New York: Bantam Books, 1973.

MUELLER, PAT, "Doing It the Hard Way," *School Arts*, January 1975, pp. 41-42.

NGUYEN, TUAN, RICHARD HESLIN, AND MICHELE L. NGUYEN, "The Meanings of Touch: Sex Differences," *Journal of Communication*, Summer 1975, pp. 92-103.

PATTISON, JOYCE E., "Effects of Touch on Self-Exploration and the Therapeutic Relationship," *Journal of Consulting and Clinical Psychology*, Vol. 40, No. 2 (1973), 170-175.

POASTER, L. B., "A Comparison of Different Modes of Communication and Their Effects on Attitude Change and the Development of

Empathy," doctoral dissertation, University of Tennessee. Ann Arbor, Mich.: University Microfilms (1971), No. 71-7669.

PRESTON, TONIE, "When Words Fail," *American Journal of Nursing,* Vol. 73, No. 12 (December 1973), 2064-2066.

SCHAFFER, H. R., AND PEGGY E. EMERSON, "Patterns of Response to Physical Contact in Early Human Development," *Journal of Child Psychology and Psychiatry,* Vol. 5 (1964), 1-13.

SMITH, SR. M. JUSTA, "Paranormal Effects on Enzyme Activity," *Human Dimensions,* 1, (1972), 15-19.

SPITZ, R. A., "Hospitalism," *The Psychoanalytic Study of the Child,* 2 (1946), 113-117.

WALKER, DAVID N., "A Dyadic Interaction Model for Nonverbal Touching Behavior in Encounter Groups," *Small Group Behavior,* Vol. 6, No. 3 (August 1975), 308-323.

———, "Openness to Touching: A Study of Strangers in Nonverbal Interaction," doctoral dissertation, University of Connecticut. Ann Arbor, Mich.: University Microfilms (1971), No. 71-18, 454.

WATSON, WILBUR H., "The Meanings of Touch: Geriatric Nursing," *Journal of Communication,* Vol. 25, 3 (Summer 1975), 104.

WEISBERG, PAUL, "Developmental Differences in Children's Preferences for High- and Low-arousing Forms of Contact Stimulation," *Child Development,* Vol. 46 (1975), 975-979.

WHITE, BURTON, L. *The First Three Years of Life.* New York: Avon Books, 1975.

WHITE, KAROL, "A Healing Power in Our Hands," *State Journal Register,* Springfield, Ill., January 15, 1979, pp. 15-16.

WINTER, RUTH, "How People React to Your Touch," *Science Digest,* March 1976, pp. 46-56.

YANG, RAYMOND K., AND THOMAS C. DOUTHITT, "Newborn Responses to Threshold Tactile Stimulation," *Child Development,* Vol. 45 (1974), 237-242.

ZASTROW, CHARLES, AND DAE H. CHANG, *The Personal Problem Solver.* Englewood Cliffs, N.J.: Prentice-Hall, 1977.

ZEFRON, LORI J., "The History of Laying-On of Hands in Nursing," *Nursing Forum,* Vol. XIV, No. 4 (1975), 350-363.

# Index

Index